*Night of Weeping*

*When God's Children Suffer*

Christian Focus Publications publishes biblically-accurate books for adults and children. The books in the adult range are published in three imprints.

*Christian Heritage* contains classic writings from the past.

*Christian Focus* contains popular works including biographies, commentaries, doctrine, and Christian living.

*Mentor* focuses on books written at a level suitable for Bible College and seminary students, pastors, and others; the imprint includes commentaries, doctrinal studies, examination of current issues, and church history.

For a free catalogue of all our titles, please write to
Christian Focus Publications,
Geanies House, Fearn,
Ross-shire, IV20 1TW, Great Britain

For details of our titles visit us on our web site
http://www.christianfocus.com

# Night of Weeping

## When God's Children Suffer

## Horatius Bonar

Christian Heritage

© Christian Focus Publications
ISBN 1 85792 441 X
Published in 1999
by
Christian Focus Publications,
Geanies House, Fearn, Ross-shire,
IV20 1TW, Great Britain.

# Contents

# PREFACE

It is no easy matter to write a book for the family of God. Yet it is for them that these thoughts on chastisement are written.

They may be found not unsuitable for the younger brethren of the Man of sorrows. For the way is rough, and the desert blast is keen. Who of them can say aught regarding their prospects here, save that tribulation awaiteth them in every place as they pass along? This they must know and prepare for, grasping more firmly at every step the gracious hand that is leading them on to the kingdom, and looking up for guidance to the loving eye that rests over them with fondest vigilance, ever bright and ever tender, whether in shadow or in sunshine, whether amid the crowds of busy life, or in the solitude of the lonely way.

It is, then, to the members of this family that this little volume is offered. They may find in it something which may not merely interest them, but may also meet their case; something, too, in which, perhaps, they may recognize, not the voice of a stranger, but of a brother: 'a companion in tribulation and in the kingdom and patience of Jesus Christ' (Rev. 1:9). For the tones of the suffering brotherhood on earth have something in them too peculiar not to be instinctively recognized. It is said of Arabian airs that they are all plaintive. They all touch some melancholy chord, as if the wail of the desert echo were the keynote of each melody. It is in some measure thus with the children of the kingdom, while sojourning in this wilderness of earth. 'Their voice is ever soft, gentle, and low.' Sorrow has smoothed away its harshness, and breathed gentler feeling into its tones. True, it is the voice of gladness, for it is the voice of the forgiven; but still it is sorrowing gladness, calm and serious joy. Their peculiar lot as followers of a hated Lord and their peculiar circumstances, as standing in the midst of a doomed and dying world, have wrought into their spirit a deep though serene solemnity of expression, alike in look and voice. Hence, there is the instinctive recognition among the brotherhood, not only of the family look, but of the family tones.

It is of family matters that we speak, and in these each member has a common interest. The 'household of faith' has many concerns, and not the least of these are its sorrows. These are the lot of all; and there is no member of the household but has his share in these, either in personal suffering or in helping to bear the burden of others.

What is now written may be found suitable to all, whether actually under chastisement or not.

It is, however, presented specially to those who are 'in heaviness through manifold temptations,' suffering the rebuke of the Lord, passing through fire and through water, with 'affliction laid upon their loins' (Ps. 66:11-12). The bruised reed must not be broken, the smoking flax must not be quenched. The hands which hang down must be lifted up, and the feeble knees confirmed; that which is lame must not be turned out of the way, but rather healed (Heb. 12:12f.).

Our desire is to minister to the saints in the consolation and admonition of the Lord. We would seek to bear their burdens, to bind up their wounds, and to dry up at least some of their many tears. To comfort those who mourn is not only to act in obedience to the command, 'Bear ye one another's burdens, and so fulfil the law of Christ'; it is to walk by the side of Jesus in His visits of mercy to His suffering saints on earth; nay, it is to be fellow-workers with the Holy Ghost as the Church's Comforter in all her tribulations and distresses.

Of these things the world knows little. Its sympathies are not with the saints, either in their sorrow or their joy. Family concerns, and especially family griefs, are not for them. And how shall they understand them so long as they remain without? They must first come in and take their place among the children beneath the paternal roof. And what should stay them? The gate stands open day and night. They would be welcomed in with the kindliest greetings of love.

But though standing afar off from the saints and unable to mingle its sympathies with theirs, the world still has sorrows of its own, deep and many. To grieve, and yet have no comforter; to be wounded, and yet have no healer; to be weary, and yet know no resting-place – this is the world's hard lot.

Yet it is a self-chosen one. God did not choose it for them. They chose it for themselves. God invites, nay, pleads earnestly with them to quit it, yet they will not. Wretched as it is, they prefer it to the friendship of Him with whom their heart is at enmity, and whose presence is to them all gloom and terror. Yet He continues to entreat them. He does not let them alone. The 'many sorrows' which compass them about are His many messages of grace, His unwearied knockings at their fast closed door. He writes 'vanity' upon the creature, 'weariness and vexation' upon earth's best delights that men may not place their confidence in these. Most mercifully does He hedge them about with disappointment of every form that they may lift their eyes above this earth and beyond these heavens to the enduring blessedness that is at His right hand forever. With what kindness, though with seeming severity, does He mar their best friendships that He may attract them to the communion of His own far better and everlasting companionship? With what compassion does He break in upon their misguided attachments that He may draw them away from earth and bind them to Himself by the more blessed ties of His own far sweeter love? With what tenderness does He tear asunder the bonds of brotherhood and kindred that He may unite them to Himself in far dearer and eternal relationship?

With what mercy does He overthrow their prospects of worldly wealth and bring down their hopes of earthly power and greatness that He may give them the heavenly treasure and make them a 'royal priesthood' to Himself in the glorious kingdom of His Son. With what love does He ruin their reputation among men, breaking in pieces their good name which was their idol that He may show them the vanity of human praise, leading them to desire the honour that cometh from God and to know that in His favour is life and that the light of His countenance is the very sunshine of Heaven.

Oh, that a weary, brokenhearted world would learn these lessons of grace! Oh, that they would taste and see that God is good! Let them but come home to Him. He will not mock them with shadows, nor feed them with husks. He will satisfy their craving souls; He will turn their midnight into noon; He will give them beauty for ashes, the oil of joy for mourning, the garment of praise for the spirit of heaviness that they may be called trees of righteousness, the planting of the Lord.

Let the world, however, regard God's dealings with them as they may: let not 'the children' despise the chastening of the Lord, nor faint when they are rebuked of Him. They at least should know the meaning of His actions toward them, for they know *Him*. The world may misunderstand His rebukes or put an unkind construction upon them; His children cannot, for they know that 'God is love'.

The thoughts that follow are designed to assist them in interpreting God's ways, not merely in finding comfort under trial, but in drawing profit from it. I have at least attempted to contribute something toward this end. I have done what I could, rather than what I would. But it may be that the Head of the family will own it, and send it with His own blessing to the scattered members near and far. He knows that they need some such words in season; and that, if thickening signs deceive not, they will ere long need them more. In such a case even this little volume may be helpful.

It is written in much weakness, and with many sins to mar it; amid what trials it is of little moment for a stranger to learn. It is written by one who is seeking himself to profit by trial, and trembles lest it should pass by as the wind over the rock, leaving it as hard as ever; by one who would fain in every sorrow draw near to God that he may know Him better, and who is not unwilling to confess that as yet he knows but little.

# 1

# THE FAMILY

It was God's *purpose* from the beginning, not merely to redeem for Himself a people out of a world of sinners, but to bring that people into a peculiar relationship to Himself. It was His purpose to draw them nearer to Himself than any other order of His creatures, and to establish a link of the closest and most peculiar kind between them and the Godhead.

To carry out this purpose was the Word made flesh. 'He took not on him the nature of angels; but he took on him the seed of Abraham' (Heb. 2:16). 'Forasmuch then as the children are partakers of flesh and blood, he also himself likewise took part of the same' (Heb. 2:14).

Thus a new relationship was established, such as till then could never have been conceived of as even possible. The tie of creation, though not dissolved, was now to be lost in the closer, dearer tie of kindred. 'Both he that sanctifieth and they who are sanctified are all of one: for which cause he is not ashamed to call them brethren' (Heb. 2:11). He calls them brethren, and they call Him Brother. Being 'made of a woman,' He has become partaker of our lowly humanity, so as to be bone of our bone, and flesh of our flesh; and we being 'born of God' are made partakers of the divine nature, becoming 'members of his body, of his flesh, and of his bones'. Thus the saints are the nearest kinsmen of the Son of God; and if of the Son, then of the Father also, as He hath said, 'I and my Father are one,' 'believest thou not that I am in the Father, and the Father in me?'

It is thus that the family relationship is formed and God's original design carried out. For thus it is written, 'As many as received him, to them gave he power [or the right] to become the sons of God, even to them that believe on his name: which were born, not of blood, nor of the will of the flesh, nor of the will of man, but of God' (John 1:12-13). And again, 'Behold, what manner of love the Father hath bestowed upon us, that we should be called the sons of God' (1 John 3:1). We are elevated to creation's highest level. We are brought into the inner circle of the Father's love – nearer His throne, nearer His heart than angels, for we are the Body of Christ, and members in particular – 'the fullness of him that filleth all in all.'

Out of this new link there springs the family bond between us and the God and Father of our Lord Jesus Christ, 'his Father and our Father, his God and our God.' And it is especially in this name of *family* that God delights. He has many names for His redeemed. They are His chosen ones, His people, His flock, His heritage. But it is as His *family* that He speaks of them oftenest, and it is, as such, that He bends over them so fondly as over His firstborn – the children of His heart and the desire of His eyes.

But it is needful that we inquire further concerning this family and learn from God's own account of them who and what they are. By nature they are children of wrath, even as others. And thus far there is no original difference between them and the world. But they are the eternally chosen of the Father, 'chosen in him [Christ] before the foundation of the world' (Eph. 1:4). This is their true ancestry, and this is their chiefest glory. They are 'predestinated ... unto the adoption of children by Jesus Christ to himself, according to the good pleasure of his will' (Eph. 1:5). They are quickened together with Christ, from being dead in trespasses and sins, and raised up by the exceeding greatness of God's power, the same mighty power by which He wrought in Christ when He raised Him from the dead (Eph. 1:19-20). They are saved by grace through faith, and that not of themselves, it is the gift of God (Eph. 2:8). They are reconciled to God by the death of His Son (Rom. 5:10). They are delivered from a present evil world according to the will of God their Father (Gal. 1:4). They are washed in the blood of Jesus and justified by faith in His name. They are redeemed from their vain conversation, not with corruptible things, as silver and gold, but with the precious blood of Christ, as of a lamb without blemish and without spot: who verily was foreordained before the foundation of the world, but was manifest in these last times for them (1 Pet. 1:18-20). They are made heirs of God, and joint-heirs with Jesus Christ, kings and priests unto God, who are to reign with Christ forever over a redeemed and restored creation.

Such is the family. Surely they are high born. Their ancestry is from eternity. Their descent is from the King of kings. They are of the blood royal of Heaven. And though their present condition be a lowly one, their prospects are the brightest that hope ever painted, brighter than what eye hath seen or ear hath heard. It doth not yet appear what they shall be; but they know that when He shall appear, they shall be like Him, for they shall see Him as He is (1 John 3:2).

But apart from these descriptions which encircle the saved family with such peculiar glory even here, their simple condition of being God's *family* calls for a little further notice. For it is not outward circumstances that form, or give interest to, a home or a family, it is the living pulse of affection that is beating there. Neither earthly pomp nor earthly poverty can materially alter the real inward character of that little circle of human hearts which man calls a family. Bright skies and sunshine cannot weaken or sever the bond; neither can they allure them away from rejoicing in each other's joy and love. Dark days and tempests cannot sunder them; they do but make them gather more closely together then, as being all in all to each other. So it is with the family of the redeemed. It is not their outward circumstances or prospects that give them the name; it is something far tenderer and deeper than these. It is the pulse of heavenly affection, throbbing through every member and coming down from the infinite heart above; it is this that makes them what they are. It is under this aspect that God delights to look upon them. It is for this reason especially that He has given to them the name they bear.

The word 'family' is a sacred one, even among the children of the world. There is a hallowed tenderness about it, which few, save the *wickedest,* do not feel in some measure. One of their own poets has thus expressed the feeling:

Beneath the foulest mother's curse
No living thing can thrive;
A mother is a mother still,
The holiest thing alive.

I am by no means in accord with the senti-ment contained in these words; the language is too strong. Still it shows the world's feeling as to the strength and sacredness of the family bond. And there is much of truth contained, or at least implied, in it. No other earthly circle can be compared with that of the family. It comprises all that a human heart most values and delights in. It is the centre where all human affections meet and entwine, the vessel into which they all pour themselves with such joyous freedom. There is no one word which contains in it so many endearing associations and precious remembrances, hidden in the heart like gold. It appeals at once to the very centre of man's being – his 'heart of hearts'. All that is sweet, soothing, tender, and true is wrapt up in that one word. It speaks not of one circle or of one bond, but of many circles and many bonds – all of them near the heart. The family home, the family hearth, the family table, family habits, family voices, family tokens, family salutations, family melodies, family joys and sorrows – what a mine of recollections lies under that one word! Take these away, and earth becomes a mere churchyard of crumbling bones; and man becomes as so many grains of loosened sand, or at best, but as the fragments of a torn flower, which the winds are scattering abroad.

All that is beautiful in human relationship, or tender in human affection, or gentle in human intercourse; all that is lovable and precious in the movements of a human heart from its lowest depth to its uppermost surface – all these are wrapt up in the one word: family. For close-knit bonds, for steadfast faithfulness in love, for depth of sympathy, for endurance in trial and danger – where shall we find anything that can be compared with the story of earth's family circles? Conjugal love, parental love, filial love, brotherly love, sisterly love – all are here. The many streams of human affection empty themselves into it, or flow out of it, for the fertility and gladness of the earth.

We need not wonder, then, that this name should be chosen as one of the Church's peculiar names. God delights in it as the name by which His company of chosen ones is to be specially called. *The Family of God* – that is the Church's name. As such He dwells in the midst of it, cares for it, and watches over it. His dealings with it are those of a father – fond yet strict – loving yet wise – sitting among His children, having His eye on each, and ordering in His gracious wisdom all the concerns of His household.

His *heart* is there! Yes, it is in His Church that God's *heart* may be said specially to be. There it unfolds itself in a way such as it can do amid no other order of His creatures. There it shows itself in all its *manifold* fullness, such as it has no scope for elsewhere. It is in the family alone that the one thing we call affection or love is divided and spread out, like a sunbeam into the rainbow's sevenfold hues, there to display itself in all the rich tints of hidden beauty. So it is in the Church alone that the love of God is fully seen, not merely in all its intensity, but in all its varied riches. All kinds of love are unfolded there. There is room for such a wide variety of affection, both between the Head and the members, and between the members one with the other, that it seems as if there had been given new powers of loving as well as new objects to love.

No doubt there are other names for the saints besides this one. But none of them expresses what this is intended to do. God calls them His *flock*, which implies tender watchfulness on His part, and dependent helplessness on theirs. He calls them a *vine*, denoting their oneness, as well as the unceasing nourishment that is ever circulating through them from the parent stem. He calls them a *temple*, signifying their compactness of structure, symmetry of design, beauty of form, and above all, fitness for the inhabitation and worship of Jehovah. He calls them a *body*, to set forth, not merely their comely proportions, but their marvellous unity and conscious vitality of being, as well as the closeness of the binding tie, and their various serviceableness to each other. He calls them a *city*, intimating their happy community of privileges and rights and well-ordered government; the security, peace, abundance which they enjoy, the comforts of neighbourhood with all its cheerful greetings and mutual offices of love. He calls them a *kingdom*, as expressive of their high and honourable estate, of the royalty, the glory, the dominion, of which they have been made the heirs.

But various and expressive as are these well-known names, they are still imperfect. They describe as it were only the outer circles, each name a circle of its own. But the inner circle – the inner region of our spiritual being – they do not touch upon. It is that well-known word, that magic name, *family,* which alone can express all that God sees of what is comely and tender, loving and lovable in the Church of Christ into which He is pouring His love, *through* which He delights to see that love circulate unhindered, and *out* of which He expects that love to flow abroad.

There is one thing that strikes us much concerning this family. It is the way in which Christ speaks of the special interest which He takes in *each* member. 'Those that thou gavest me I have kept, and none of them is lost' (John 17:12). How like the family feeling! Each name, each face is known; known so familiarly that the least and youngest would at once be missed. The place where each sits, the room which each occupies, the time of his going out and coming in; his looks, his habits, his tones are so thoroughly known that the moment anyone is absent, he is missed. And then no other can supply his place. His absence makes a blank which none but he can fill. An acquaintance or fellow-townsman may drop away and never be missed. His place is easily filled by another. Not so with a member of the family. Where there is a break in the circle, there is a dismal blank; and when death has carried off a brother, a sister, or a parent, who or what can ever fill his room? When one flower fades, another springs up, fresher perhaps and more fragrant – and we forget the faded one. But the withered family flower can have no successor: it dies, and there is a blank forever. Might it not be with some such feeling that Jesus looked around upon His vast household circle, and, while surveying each well-known face, gave thanks that not one was lost; as if He could not have spared so much as one of those whom the Father had given Him.

Oh, the deep interest which Jesus takes in *each!* Truly it is a personal and peculiar attachment for each member. Do we not lose much by forgetting this? Even in human things we are apt to overlook this. We call the feeling which the Father entertains for each of His children, love; and well we call it so, but this is not all. There is a difference in the love He bears for His eldest and His youngest born, a difference in the case of each, called forth by the peculiar character of each. It is this minute and special love which is so precious. Were it not for this, we should feel as if we had only part of our Father's heart, as if we had not all of that which rightfully belongs to us. But, realizing this, we feel as if we had His whole heart, and yet our having the whole did not rob our brothers and sisters of any. It is with a family as with the sun in the firmament. It is the property of all, and yet each has the whole of it. Even so with Jehovah, our heavenly Father; even so with Jesus, our Elder Brother. His is a special, personal, peculiar love, just as if He loved no other, but had His whole heart to spare for us. His is a minute and watchful care, bending over *each,* day and night, as if He had no other to care for. How sweet to think that each of us is the special object of such personal attachment, the peculiar object of such unwearied vigilance! What manner of love is this! Now we believe and are sure that we shall be fully cared for, and not one want or sorrow will be overlooked. Now we know that 'all things shall work together for our good,' and that the end of everything which befalls us here shall be light and glory forever! 'I know the thoughts that I think towards you, saith the Lord, thoughts of peace and not of evil, to give you an expected end' (Jer. 29:11). 'As one whom his mother comforteth, so will I comfort you' (Isa. 66:13). 'Like as a father pitieth his children, so the Lord pitieth them that fear him' (Ps. 103:13).

It is sweet to realize the common love flowing

out of the Father's bosom to the whole happy household of His saved ones; but it is no less sweet, specially in the day of trial, to dwell upon the personal love He bears so peculiarly to each. It is blessed to identify ourselves with such a family who are all joying in the sunshine of paternal love; but it is as blessed at times to isolate oneself and realize the individual love which is our own peculiar heritage. Thus felt the Bride when she said, 'Let him kiss me with the kisses of his mouth: for thy love is better than wine' (Song 1:2). 'I am my beloved's, and my beloved is mine' (Song 6:3).

It was when the Holy Spirit first opened our ears to listen to the tale of love which the gospel brought to us that we sought our Father's house and rested not until we had found ourselves in His embrace. It was when we first received 'the gift of God,' and understood the love which that gift declared, that we took our place in the family circle, tasting the plenty of our Father's table and enjoying the sweetness of our Father's smile. And even as we entered in, so are we to abide forever, 'rooted and grounded in love,' realizing the words of Jesus, 'As the Father hath loved me, so have I loved you: *continue ye in my love*' (John 15:9).

# 2

# THE FAMILY LIFE

They live by *faith*. Thus they began and thus they are to end. 'We walk by faith and not by sight.' Their whole life is a life of faith, their daily actions are all of faith. This forms one of the main elements of their character. It marks them out as a peculiar people. None live as they do.

Their faith is to them 'the substance of things hoped for, the evidence of things not seen'. It is a sort of substitute for sight and possession. It so brings them into contact with the unseen world that they feel as if they were already conversant with, and living among, the things unseen. It makes the future, the distant, the impalpable, appear as the present, the near, the real. It removes all intervening time; it annihilates all interposing space; it transplants the soul at once into the world above. That which we know is to be hereafter is felt as if already in being. Hence, the coming of the Lord is always spoken of as at hand. Nay, more than this, the saints are represented as 'having their conversation in heaven,' as being already 'seated with Christ in heavenly places' (Eph. 2:6), as having 'come to Mount Zion, and unto the city of the living God, the heavenly

Jerusalem, and to an innumerable company of angels, to the general assembly and church of the firstborn, which are written in heaven, and to God the Judge of all, and to the spirits of just men made perfect' (Heb. 12:22-23). The things amid which they are to move hereafter are so realized by faith as to appear the things amid which they are at present moving. They sit in 'heavenly places' and look down upon the earth, with all its clouds and storms, as lying immeasurably far beneath their feet. And what is a 'present evil world' to those who are already above all its vicissitudes and breathing a purer atmosphere?

Such is the power of faith. It throws back into the far distance the things of earth, the things that men call near and real; and it brings forward into vital contact with the soul the things which men call invisible and distant. It discloses to us the heavenly mansions, their passing splendour, their glorious purity, their blessed peace. It shows us the happy courts, the harmonious company, the adoring multitudes. It opens our ears also, so that when beholding these great sights we seem to hear the heavenly melody and to catch the very words of the new song they sing, 'Thou art worthy … for thou wast slain, and hast redeemed us to God by thy blood out of every kindred, and tongue, and people and nation; and hast made us unto our God kings and priests: and we shall reign on the earth' (Rev. 5:9-10).

It, moreover, points our eye forward to what is yet to come: the coming of the Lord, the judgment of the great day, the restitution of all things, the kingdom that cannot be moved, the city which hath foundations whose builder and maker is God. While thus it gives to things invisible a body and a form which before they possessed not in our eyes, on the other hand, it divests things visible of that semblance of excellence and reality with which they were formerly clothed. It strips the world of its false but bewildering glow, and enables us to penetrate the thin disguise that hides its poverty and meanness. It not only sweeps away the cloud which hung above us, obstructing our view of heavenly excellence, but it places that cloud beneath us to counteract the fallacious brightness and unreal beauty which the world has thrown over itself to mask its inward deformity.

Thus it is that faith enables us to realize our true position of pilgrims and strangers upon earth, looking for the city which hath foundations, whose builder and maker is God. It is into this that we are introduced by faith at our conversion. For what is our conversion but a turning of our back upon the world and bidding farewell to all that the heart had hitherto been entwined around? It is then that like Abraham we forsake all and go out not knowing whither. Old ties are broken, although sometimes hard to sever. New ones are formed, although not of earth. We begin to look around us and find all things new. We feel that we are strangers – strangers in that very spot where we have been so long at home. But this is our joy. We have left our father's house, but we are hastening on to a more enduring home. We have taken leave of the world – but we have become heirs of the eternal kingdom, sons and daughters of the Lord Almighty. We have left Egypt, but Canaan is in view. We are in the wilderness, but we are free. Ours is a pathless waste, but we move forward under the shadow of the guardian cloud. Sorrowful, we yet rejoice; poor, we make many rich; having nothing, yet we possess all things. We have a rich inheritance in reversion and a long eternity in which to enjoy it without fear of loss, or change, or end.

Walking thus by faith and not by sight, what should move us? What should mar our joy? Does it not come from that which is within the veil? And what storm of the desert can find entrance there? Our rejoicing is in the Lord, and He is without variableness or shadow of turning. We know that this is not our rest; neither do we wish it were so, for it is polluted; but our joy is this, that Jehovah is our God, and His promised glory is our inheritance forever. Our morning and our evening song is this, 'The LORD is the portion of mine inheritance and of my cup: thou maintainest my lot. The lines have fallen unto me in pleasant places; yea, I have a goodly heritage' (Ps. 16:5-6).

Why should we, then, into whose hands the cup of gladness shall ere long be put, shrink from the vinegar and the gall? Why should we, who have dearer friends above, better bonds that cannot be dissolved, be disconsolate at the severance of an earthly tie? Our homes may be empty, our firesides may be thinned, and our hearts may bleed: but these are not enduring things; and why should we feel desolate as if all gladness had departed? Why should we, who shall wear a crown and inherit all things, sigh or fret because of a few years' poverty and shame? Earth's dream will soon be done; and then comes the day of 'songs and everlasting joy' – the long reality of bliss! Jesus will soon be here; and 'when he who is our life shall appear, then shall we also appear with him in glory'.

Shall trial shake us? Nay, in all this we are more than conquerors through Him that loved us. Shall sorrow move us? Faith tells us of a land where sorrow is unknown. Shall the death of saints move us? Faith tells us not to sorrow as those who have no hope, for if we believe that Jesus died and rose again, them also that sleep in Jesus will God bring with Him. Shall the pains and weariness of this frail body move us? Faith tells us of a time at hand when this corruptible shall put on incorruption, and death shall be swallowed up in victory. Shall privation move us? Faith tells us of a day when the poverty of our exile shall be forgotten in the abundance of our peaceful, plenteous home, where we shall hunger no more, neither thirst any more.

Shall the disquieting bustle of this restless life annoy us? Faith tells us of the rest that remaineth for the people of God – the sea of glass like unto crystal on which the ransomed saints shall stand – no tempest, no tumult, no shipwreck there. Shall the lack of this world's honours move us? Faith tells us of the exceeding and eternal weight of glory in reserve. Have we no place to lay our head? Faith tells us that we have a home, though not in Caesar's house, a dwelling, though not in any city of earth. Are we fearful as we look around upon the disorder and wretchedness of this misgoverned earth? Faith tells us that the coming of the Lord draweth nigh. Do thoughts of death alarm us? Faith tells us that 'to die is gain,' and whispers to us, 'What, are you afraid of becoming immortal, afraid of passing from this state of death, which men call life, to that which alone truly deserves the name!'

Such is the family life – a life of faith. We live upon things unseen. Our life is hid with Christ in God that when He who is our life shall appear, we may appear with Him in glory. This mode of life is not that of the world at all but the very opposite. Nevertheless, it has been that of the saints from the beginning. This is the way in which they have walked, going up through the wilderness leaning on their Beloved. And such is to be the walk of the saints till the Lord comes. Oh, how much is there in these thoughts concerning it, not only to reconcile us to it, but to make us rejoice in it, and to say, I reckon that the sufferings of this present life, are not worthy to be compared with the glory which shall be revealed in us! For all things are ours, whether life or death, things present or things to come, all are ours; for we are Christ's, and Christ is God's. Yea, we are heirs of God, and joint-heirs with Jesus Christ. 'This is the heritage of the servants of the LORD, and their righteousness is of me, saith the LORD' (Isa. 54:17).

We know not a better type or specimen of the family life than Abraham or Israel in their desert wanderings. Look at Abraham. He quits all at the command of the God of glory. This begins his life of faith. Then he journeys onward not knowing whither. Then he sojourns as a stranger in the land which God had given him. Then he offers up Isaac. Then he buys for himself a tomb where he may lay his dust till the day of resurrection. All is faith. He lives and acts as a stranger. He has no home. He has his altar and his tent, but that is all – the one he builds wherever he goes, in the peaceful consciousness of sin forgiven and acceptance found; the other he pitches from day to day in token of his being a pilgrim and a stranger upon earth. And what more does any member of the family need below, but his altar and his tent – a Saviour for a sinful soul, and a shelter for a frail body until journeying days are done?

Or look at Israel. They quit Egypt. There the life of faith begins. Then they cross the Red Sea. Then they take up their abode in the desert. They have no city to dwell in now. They have no fleshpots now – nothing but the daily manna for food. They have no river of Egypt now – nothing but a rock to yield them water. All is waste around. All is to be faith, not of sight. They are alone with God, and the whole world is afar off. They rear their altar, they pitch their tents, as did Abraham, with this only difference; above their heads there floats a wondrous cloud, which, like a heavenly canopy, stretches itself out over their dwellings when they rest, or like an angel-guide, it takes wing before them when God summons them to strike their tents that it may lead them in the way. Nay, and as if to mark more vividly the pilgrim condition of the family, God Himself, when coming down into the midst of them, chooses a *tent* to dwell in. It is called 'the tabernacle of the Lord,' or more literally 'Jehovah's tent'. Jehovah pitches His tent side by side with Israel's tents, as if He were a stranger too, a wanderer like themselves!

This is our life. We are to be strangers with

God as all our fathers were. It is the life of the desert, not of the city. But what of that? All is well. Jehovah is our God, and we shall soon be in His 'many mansions'. Meanwhile, we have the tent, the altar, and the cloud. We need no more below. The rest is secured for us in Heaven, 'ready to be revealed in the last time.'

# 3

# THE FAMILY BADGE

The family of which we speak is gathered out of every nation and kindred, and people, and tongue. It is 'a great multitude that no man can number'.

Yet it is but *one* family. There is a family likeness among all its members; and a family name by which they are known. They have many things in common; nay, there are few things which are not common to all. They are all sprinkled with the same blood and begotten again by the same Spirit. They all sing one song, use one language, rejoice in one hope, and are heirs of one inheritance. This oneness of feature and feeling and habit, throughout so many ages and amid so many diverse nations, marks them out as a peculiar people and reveals their relationship to Him who is 'the same yesterday, and today and forever'.

But they have one mark more peculiar than any of these. It is truly a family badge; they are all *cross-bearers*. This is the unfailing token by which each member may be recognized. They all bear a cross. Nor do they hide it as if ashamed of it. They make it their boast. 'God forbid that we should glory, save in the cross of our Lord

Jesus Christ, by whom the world is crucified to us, and we unto the world' (Gal. 6:14). Sometimes it is lighter, and sometimes it is heavier; sometimes it has more of shame and suffering, and sometimes less, but still it is upon them. They carry it with them wherever they go. And it is always *a cross:* not merely so in name, but in reality, a token of reproach and sorrow. Sometimes they are represented as carrying it, and sometimes as being nailed to it, but it is still the *cross.*

They took it up when first they believed in Jesus and owned Him as their all. Then it was that they forsook the world's tents and went without the gate, bearing the reproach of the crucified One. He whom they follow both bore the cross and was nailed to it, and why should they shrink from the like endurance? Shall they be ashamed of Him? Shall they not rather count it honourable to follow where He has led the way, and to bear for Him some faint resemblance of what He bore for them? Shall anything in the world be esteemed more precious, more honourable than the cross of their beloved Lord? The world derides and despises it, but it is the cross of Jesus; and that is *all* to them. A saint of other days, a cross-bearer of the olden time, has said, 'O blessed cross of Christ, there is no wood like thine!'

Besides, this was the Master's will. He has laid on each the *command* to bear the cross. 'If any man will come after me, let him deny himself, and take up his cross daily, and follow me' (Luke 9:23). 'He that taketh not his cross, and followeth after me, is not worthy of me' (Matt. 10:38). The cross, then, is the badge of discipleship, and no follower of the Lord can be without it. The two things are inseparable. God has joined them, and man cannot sunder them. No cross, no saint. No cross, no Son. We must carry His cross all our life; we must be baptized with His baptism; we must endure His reproach; we must glory in being clothed with His shame. The flesh must be crucified with its affections and lusts: our members must be mortified; our old man must take the place of shame; we in whom the flesh still remaineth though its dominion is broken, must be willing to appear as outcasts and malefactors before the world, as Jesus did when He bore our sins upon the hill of shame. Jesus, then, with His own hand lays the cross on each one who comes to Him, saying, 'Take this and follow Me. Take it and be reproached for Me. Take it and endure tribulation for Me. Take it, and count all things but loss for the excellency of the knowledge of Jesus Christ thy Lord. Take it and be willing to go even to prison or to death for Me, not counting your life dear unto you, that you may follow Me to the end and receive the unfading crown.' Learn to endure the cross and to despise the shame.

But further, we have the Master's *example* as well as the Master's will concerning this. I do not mean merely that He hung upon the cross. I do not refer simply to the fact of His crucifixion. I mean much more than that. That was but the closing scene of a whole life of crucifixion. He was a cross-bearer from the hour that He was laid in the manger. All His days He bore the cross. His life was but a pilgrimage to Calvary with the cross upon His shoulders. Tradition tells us that, as He left the Judgment hall, He was led along the *'dolorous* way' to Golgotha. But in truth, His whole course on earth was the mournful way. It was all reproach and sorrow from His cradle to His grave. His was a sorrowing life; His death was but the summing up of His many sorrows, the gathering of them altogether and pressing them into His cup at once, till the vessel burst, because it could hold no more. And then, for Him, the cross and the shame and the sorrow were at an end forever. But for us the cross remaineth still.

Throughout life He was the 'man of sorrows'. He was 'acquainted with grief.' And herein we see something more of the family badge as it was displayed in the Elder Brother. Acquaintanceship with grief! This is the description given us of it. It is not one visit that makes us acquainted with a fellowman. Companionship is the result of continued intercourse. So one sorrow does not make us acquainted with grief, however deep and sharp its pangs may be. It may be the beginning of our acquaintanceship, but that is all. There must be daily, hourly intercourse. Thus it was with Jesus. Thirty-three years daily converse with grief made Him acquainted with it. And so it is with us. The saints are men of sorrows still; and their acquaintanceship with grief must be obtained by daily fellowship. The disciple is not above his Master, nor the servant above his Lord. We need not think of another process than that which He underwent. He was made perfect through sufferings, and so must we. The Captain of our salvation is, in this respect, the model and pattern of His saved ones. We are always to bear 'about in the body the dying of the Lord Jesus, that the life also of Jesus might be made manifest in our body' (2 Cor. 4:10).

It is the Lamb that we follow: the Lamb 'as it had been slain'. This surely speaks most plainly of the family badge. We are followers of the Man with the pierced hands and feet, the Man who is covered all over with the marks of the buffet and the scourge and the spitting, the Man with the crown of thorns. Yea, He is our Elder Brother. He is bone of our bone and flesh of our flesh. And if we see so distinctly the family badge on Him, shall we shrink from taking it up and binding it in triumph as a jewel on our forehead – as a crown upon our head? Surely the purple robe of mockery may beseem us better than it suited Him.

There is one mark by which, from the beginning, He has been distinguished as the woman's seed predicted in Eden. It is the *bruised heel*. This is, in truth, only another way of expressing His character as the suffering, the crucified Son of Man. This was the mark which God gave by which He was to be known. Yet it was just at this stumbling stone that Israel stumbled. They had no eyes for the dying Saviour. The humbled Jesus found no favour with them. The bruised heel they could not away with. The very mark which God set upon Him as Messiah was that on account of which Israel rejected Him. Yet it is the bruised heel in which we rejoice. It is the Man with the bruised heel who has won our hearts. It is He whom we follow; and His bruised heel we engrave upon our banner as our most honourable badge.

The similar bruising we look for as our portion here. Nor are we ashamed of it. All the saints before us have experienced it; are we better than they? Shall the soldiers of the last days be ashamed to wear the uniform which the arm of the saints has gloried in for six thousand years?

It is very remarkable that the apostle fixes upon affliction as the mark of true Sonship. Truly, he makes it the family badge. Nay, he makes it the test of our legitimacy. 'What son is he whom the father chasteneth not? But if ye be without chastisement, whereof all are partakers, then are ye bastards, and not sons' (Heb. 12:7-8). Strong language this! Had any but an inspired apostle used it, there would have been outcry against it as absurd and extravagant. Let us, however, take it as it is, for we know that it speaks the mind of God. Chastisement is, then, really one of the chief marks of our lawful and honourable birth. Were this characteristic not to be found on us, we should be lacking in one of the proofs of our sonship. Our legitimacy might be called in question. It might be said that He was not recognizing us as His true-born sons, and that either He had never received us as such, or had rejected us. There must be the family badge to establish our claim of birth and to be a pledge of paternal recognition on the part of God our Father.

It is a solemn thought. Flesh and blood shrink from it. We look around to see if there be no way of escaping, and ask if it must be so. Yes, it must be, as we shall shortly see, and the attempt to shun it is vain. Yet it is also a blessed thought. It cheers us under trial to remember that this is the Father's seal set upon His true-born sons. Oh! how it lightens the load to think that it is really the pledge of our divine adoption.

We need not then count upon bright days below, nor think to pass lightly over the pleasant earth as if our life were but the 'shadow of a dream'. Joy *within* we may expect – 'joy unspeakable and full of glory' – for that is the family portion. But joy from without, the joy of earth's sunshine, the joy of the world's ease and abundance, the joy of unsevered bonds and unweeping eyes is not our lot in this vale of tears.

Still, in the midst of the ever-wakeful storms through which we are passing to the kingdom, there is peace – deep peace – too deep for any storm of earth to reach. In the world we have tribulation, but in Jesus we have peace. 'Peace I leave with you, my peace I give unto you, not as the world giveth, give I unto you' (John 14:27). And it is this which gives the peculiar aspect to the saints, the aspect of mingled joy and grief. The eye is dim with tears, yet, behold! it glistens with joy. There is the brow of shaded thought, yet peace is playing round it. Clouds overshadow them, but on every cloud we see calm sunshine resting.

Their 'peace is like a river'. It is not stagnant as the lake, nor tumultuous as the sea, but ever in calm motion, ever flowing on in its deep channel like a river. The course may sometimes be through rocks, sometimes through level plains, sometimes through tangled brakes, sometimes along the cornfield or 'the hill of vines,' yet still it moves unhindered on. It may be night or day, it may be winter or summer, it may be storm or calm, but it is there – flowing on till the embrace of ocean receives it. Such is our peace! Let us hold it fast.

Nor need we hide our peace any more than we should hide our cross. Let the world see both and learn how well they agree together. For it is the cross that makes this peace feel so sweet and suitable. Amid the tears of grief peace keeps her silent place like the rainbow upon the spray of the cataract; nor can it be driven thence so long as Jehovah's sunshine rests upon the soul. 'The work of righteousness shall be peace, and the effect of righteousness, quietness and assurance forever.'

# 4

# THE FAMILY DISCIPLINE

'Train up a child in the way he should go' is the injunction God lays on us. But it is, moreover, the principle on which He Himself is acting with His Church. He is training up His children here. This is the true character of His dealings with them. The education of His saints is the object He has in view. It is training for the kingdom; it is education for eternity.

How momentous, then, is the training! It is God who is carrying it on by the Holy Ghost. It is the Church, which is the Body of Christ, that is the subject of it. And it is to prepare her for an everlasting kingdom! In bringing many sons unto glory, it was needful that even the Captain of their salvation should be made perfect through suffering. Surely, then, God lays vast stress upon this discipline. In His estimation it is no unimportant nor unmeaning exercise. Knowing this, the apostle exhorts us on this very point, 'My son, despise not thou the chastening of the Lord.' It is too solemn to be despised, too momentous to be overlooked. The education of God's family is concerned with it. The preparation of an heir of glory depends on it.

This discipline begins at our conversion. The moment we are taken into the family it commences. 'He scourgeth every son whom he receiveth.' It is not always visible; neither are we at all times conscious of its operation. Nevertheless, from the very day that 'we are begotten again to a lively hope' it begins.

It ends only with life, or in the case of the last generation of the Church, with their being 'caught up to meet the Lord in the air'. It is a whole life-time's process. It is a daily, an hourly discipline which admits of no cessation. The rod may not always be applied, but still the discipline goes on.

*1. It is the discipline of love.* Every step of it is kindness. There is no wrath or vengeance in any part of the process. The discipline of the school may be harsh and stern, but that of the family is love. We are sure of this; and the consolation which it affords is unutterable. Love will not wrong us. There will be no needless suffering. Were this but kept in mind there would be fewer hard thoughts of God among men, even when His strokes are most severe. I know not a better illustration of what the feelings of a saint should be, in the hour of bitterness, than the case of Richard Cameron's father. The aged saint was in prison 'for the Word of God and the testimony of Jesus Christ'. The bleeding head of his martyred son was brought to him by his unfeeling persecutors, and he was asked derisively if he knew it. 'I know it, I know it,' said the father, as he kissed the mangled forehead of his fair-haired son, 'it is my son's; my own dear son's! It is the Lord! Good is the will of the Lord, who cannot wrong me or mine, but who hath made goodness and mercy to follow us all our days.'

2. *It is the discipline of wisdom.* He who administers it is the 'God only wise'. What deep wisdom then must there be in all His dealings! He knows exactly what we need and how to supply it. He knows what evils are to be found in us, and how these may be best removed. His training is no random work. It is carried on with exquisite skill. The time and the way and the instrument are all according to the perfect wisdom of God. The fittest time is chosen, just the very moment when discipline is called for, and when it would be most profitable. The surest, most direct, and at the same time gentlest method is devised. The instrument which will be surest yet safest, most effectual yet least painful, is brought into operation. For all is wisdom in the discipline of God.

3. *It is the discipline of faithfulness.* 'In faithfulness thou hast afflicted me,' said David. All is the doing of a faithful God – a God who is faithful to us as well as faithful to Himself. 'Faithful are the wounds of a friend,' says Solomon; and the believer finds in trouble the

faithfulness of the truest of friends. He is so faithful that He will not pass by a single fault that He sees in us, but will forthwith make it known that it may be removed. He gave this command to Israel, 'Thou shalt in any wise rebuke thy neighbour, and not suffer sin upon him' (Lev. 19:17), and He Himself acts upon the command He gave. He is too faithful a Father to suffer sin upon His children unreproved. He is true to us, whether in sending the evil or the good; shall we not say, truer and more faithful when He inflicts the evil than when He bestows the good? It almost at times seems to break the heart of a loving friend to be obliged to say or do anything severe toward the friend he loves. Yet for love's sake he will do it. In faithfulness he will not shrink from it. And in doing so, is he not true to his friend? So with a chastening God. He is faithful when He blesses – more faithful when He chastens. This surely is consolation. It may well allay all murmuring and establish our hearts in peace.

4. *It is the discipline of power.* He who is carrying it on is not one who can be baffled and forced to give up His design. He is able to carry it out in the unlikeliest circumstances and against the most resolute resistance. Everything must give way before Him. This thought is, I confess, to me one of the most comforting connected with the discipline. If it could fail! If God could be

48

frustrated in His designs after we have suffered so much, it would be awful! To be scourged and suffer pain by one who is not able to make good to us the profit of this would add inconceivable bitterness to the trial. And then our hearts are so hard, our wills so stubborn, that nothing save an Almighty pressure applied to them can work the desired change. Oh, when the soul is at strife within itself, battling in desperate conflict with its stormy lusts, when the flesh rises up in its strength and refuses to yield, when the whole heart appears like iron or is adamant, it is most blessed to think upon God's chastisements as the discipline of power! It is this that assures us that all shall yet be well. And it is in the strength of this assurance that we gird ourselves for the battle, knowing that we must be more than conquerors through Him that loved us.

There might be love in the dealing – love to the uttermost – and yet all be in vain. For love is oftentimes helpless, unable to do aught for the beloved object. There might be wisdom, too, and yet it might prove wholly ineffectual. There might also be untiring faithfulness, yet no results. It might be baffled in its most earnest attempts to bless. But when it is infinite power that is at work, we are sure of every obstacle being surmounted, and everything that is blessed coming most surely to pass. My sickbed may be most lovingly tended, most skilfully provided for, most faithfully watched, and I may be most sweetly soothed by this fond and unwearied care; yet, if there be no power to heal, no resistless energy such as sweeps all hindrances before it, then I may still lie hopeless there; but, if the power to heal be present, the power that makes all diseases flee its touch, the power that, if need be, can raise the dead, then I know of a truth that all is well.

Oh, it is blessed and comforting to remember that it is the discipline of *power* that is at work upon us! God's treatment *must* succeed. It cannot miscarry or be frustrated even in its most arduous efforts, even in reference to its minutest objects. It is the mighty power of God that is at work within us and upon us, and this is our consolation. It is the grasp of an infinite hand that is upon us, and nothing can resist its pressure. All is love, all is wisdom, and all is faithfulness, yet all is also *power.* The very possibility of failure is thus taken away. Were it not for this *power* there could be no certainty of blessing, and were it not for this *certainty,* how poor and partial would our comfort be! He, yes, He who chastises us 'is *able* to do exceeding abundantly above all that we ask or think, according to the power that worketh in us' (Eph. 3:20).

Hence to a soul, conscious of utter helplessness and weary of the struggle within, between the spirit and the flesh, there is 'strong consolation' in remembering the *power* of Him whose hand is now grasping him so firmly on every side. His sorely tossed spirit finds peace in calling to mind 'the years of the right hand of the Most High' – all the 'works of the Lord and his wonders of old'. The 'strength of Israel' is the name he delights in, as the name of his Chastener. He thus bethinks himself, 'The God who made these heavens and stretched them out in their vastness and majesty, who moves these stars in their courses and arrests them at a word, is the God who is chastening me. He who raises and stills the mighty deep and all the multitude of its waves, the God of the tempest and of the earthquake, "the framer of light and dark, the wielder of the lightning and the builder of the everlasting hills," is the God who is now laying His rod so heavily upon me.' Thus each new proof or aspect of Jehovah's power becomes a new source of consolation in the day of chastisement and sorrow.

Such, then, is the nature of the family discipline when viewed in reference to God. Love, wisdom, faithfulness, and power unite to devise and carry it out. It must, then, be *perfect* discipline, the completest and most successful that can be thought of or desired. It is well to look at it in this light, for it is thus that we become entirely satisfied with all that comes to pass and feel that 'it is well'. But let us consider it in another aspect. We have seen what it is when flowing out of God; let us see what it is when operating upon man.

As we observed before, God's object in chastisement is the *education* of His children, the training up of the saints. It is their imperfect spiritual condition that makes this so necessary. And now we proceed to inquire in what way it works, and toward what regions of the soul it is specially directed. For while, doubtless, it embraces the whole soul in all its parts and powers, it may be well to consider it as more especially set to work upon its mind, its will, its heart, and its conscience.

*1. It is the training of the mind.* We are naturally most unteachable as well as most ignorant, neither knowing anything nor willing to know. The ease of prosperous days augments the evil. God at length interposes and compels us to learn. 'The rod and reproof give wisdom' (Prov. 29:15). He sends trial and that makes us willing to learn. Our unteachableness gives way. We become aware of our ignorance. We seek teaching from on high. God begins His work of instruction. Light pours in on every side. We grow amazingly in knowledge. We learn the meaning of words now which we had hitherto used but as familiar sounds. Scripture shines out before us in new effulgence; it flashes into us; every verse seems to contain a sunbeam; dark places become light; every promise stands out in illuminated splendour; things hard to be understood become in a moment plain.

How fast we learn in a day of sorrow! It is as if affliction awoke our powers and lent them new quickness of perception. We advance more in the knowledge of Scripture in a single day than in years before. We learn 'songs in the night,' though such music was unknown before. A deeper experience has taken us down into the depths of Scripture and shown us its hidden wonders. Luther used to say, 'Were it not for tribulation I should not understand Scripture.' And every sorrowing saint responds to this, as having felt its truth – felt it as did David, when he said, 'Blessed is the man whom thou chastenest, ... and teachest him out of thy law' (Ps. 94:12). 'It is good for me that I have been afflicted; that I might learn thy statutes' (Ps. 119:71). What teaching, what training of the mind goes on upon a sickbed, or under the pressure of grief! And, oh, what great and wondrous things will even some little trial whisper in the ear of a soul that is 'learning of the Father'!

In some cases this profit is almost unfelt, at least during the continuance of the process. We think that we are learning nothing. Sorrow overwhelms us. Disaster stuns us. We become confused, nervous, agitated, or perhaps insensible. We seem to derive no profit. Yet ere long we begin to feel the blessed results. Maturity of judgment, patience in listening to the voice of God, a keener appetite for His Word, a quicker discernment of its meaning – these are soon realized as the gracious results of chastisement. The mind has undergone a most thorough discipline, and has, moreover, made wondrous progress in the knowledge of divine truth through the teaching of the Holy Ghost.

*2. It is the training of the will.* The will is the seat of rebelliousness. Here the warfare is carried on. 'The flesh lusteth against the spirit, and the spirit against the flesh.' At conversion the will is bent in the right direction, but it is still crooked and rigid. Rebelliousness is still there. Prosperous days may sometimes conceal it so that we are almost unconscious of its strength. But it still exists. Furnace heat is needed for softening and strengthening it. No milder remedy will do. 'It requires,' says a suffering saint, 'all the energy of God to bend my will to His.' Yet it must be done. The will is the soul's citadel. Hence, it is the *will* that God seems so specially to aim at in chastisement. Fire after fire does He kindle in order to soften it; blow after blow does He fetch down on it to straighten it. Nor does He rest till He has made it thoroughly flexible and hammered out of it the many relics of self which it contains. He will not stay His hand till He has thoroughly marred our self-formed plans and shown us the folly of our self-chosen ways.

This is specially the case in long-continued trials; either when these come stroke after stroke in sad succession, or when one fearful stroke at the outset has left behind it consequences which years perhaps will not fully unfold. The bending and straightening of the will is often a long process, during which the soul has to pass through waters deep and many, through fires hot and ever kindling up anew. Protracted trials seem specially aimed at the *will*. Its perversity and stiffness can only be wrought out of it by a long succession of trials. It is only by degrees that it becomes truly pliable and is brought into harmony with the will of God. We can at a stroke lop off the unseemly branch; but to give a proper *bent* to the tree itself, we require time and assiduous appliances for months or years. Yet the will must give way. However proud, however forward, it must bend. God will not leave it till He has made it one with His own.[1]

*3. It is the training of the heart.* Man's heart beats *false* to God. It is true to many things but false to Him. When first the Holy Spirit touches it, and shows it 'the exceeding riches of the grace of God,' then it becomes in some measure *true*. Yet it is only in part. Much falseheartedness still remains. It clings too fondly to the creature. It cleaves to the dust. It is not wholly God's. But

---

1. 'Character is a perfectly educated will,' says a German writer.

this cannot be. God must have the heart; nay, and He must have it beating truly toward Him. He is jealous of our love, and grieves over its feebleness or its falling away. It is love that He wants, and with nothing but true-hearted love will He be satisfied. For this it is that He chastises.

These false throbbings of the heart; these goings out after other objects than Himself He cannot suffer but must correct or else forego His claim. Hence, He smites and spares not till He has made us sensible of our guilt in this respect. He strips off the leaves whose beauty attracted us; He cuts down the flowers whose fragrance fascinated us; He tears off one string after another from the lyre whose music charmed us. Then when He has showed us each object of earth in its nakedness or deformity, then He presents Himself to us in the brightness of His own surpassing glory. And thus He wins the heart. Thus He makes it true to Him. Thus He makes us ashamed of our falseheartedness to Himself and to the Son of His love.

Yet this is no easy process. This training is hard and sore. The heart bleeds under it. Yet it must go on. No part of it can be spared. Nor will it cease till the heart is won! If the Chastener should stay His hand before this is effected, where would be His love? What poor, what foolish affection! He knew this when He said, 'Let them alone'; and it was the last thing that His love consented to do, after all else had failed. One of the sharpest, sorest words He ever spoke to Israel was, 'Why should ye be stricken any more?' Let us remember this, and not faint, even though the heart has been long bleeding. Let us remember it, and seek to make the sorrow shorter by gladly joining with Him in His plan for getting possession of our whole heart. We need not grudge it. He has 'good measure' to give us in return. His love will taste the sweeter, and it will abide and satisfy us forever. It is well for us to be thus trained to love Him here, with whom, in love and fellowship unbroken, we are to spend the everlasting day.

*4. It is the training of the conscience.* A seared conscience is the sinner's heritage. It is upon this that the Holy Spirit first lays His hand when He awakens the soul from its sleep of death. He touches the conscience, and then the struggles of conviction come. He then pacifies it by the sprinkling of the blood, showing it Jesus and His cross. Then giving it to taste forgiveness, it rests from all its tumults and fears. Thoughts of peace are ever breathed into it from the sight of the bleeding sacrifice. It trembles no more, for it sees that that which made it tremble is the very thing concerning which the blood of Christ speaks peace. 'Their sins and their iniquities will I remember no more.' Thus it is softened. Its first terrors upon awakening could not be called a softening. But now conscious forgiveness and realized peace with God have been to it like the mild breath of spring to the ice of winter. It has become soft and tender. Yet only so in part.

God's desire, however, is to make it altogether tender. He wishes it to be sensitive in regard to the very touch of sin, and earnest in its pantings after perfect holiness. To effect this, He afflicts; and affliction goes directly home to the conscience. The death of the widow's son at Sarepta immediately awakened her conscience, and she cried to the prophet, 'O man of God, art thou come to call my sin to remembrance?' (1 Kings 17:18). So God by chastisement lays His finger upon the conscience, and forthwith it springs up into new life. We are made to feel as if God had now come down to us, as if He were now looking into our hearts and commencing a narrow search. Moreover, we see in this affliction God's estimate of sin. Not, indeed, the full estimate. No, that we only learn from the sufferings of Jesus. But still we gather from this new specimen of sin's bitter fruits somewhat of His mind regarding sin. This *teaches* the conscience by making the knowledge of sin a thing of experience – an experience that is deepening with every new trial. 'If they be bound in fetters, and be holden in cords of affliction; then he showeth them their work, and their transgressions that they have exceeded. He openeth also their ear to discipline, and commandeth that they return from iniquity' (Job 36:8-10).

In these last days how little is there of tenderness of conscience! The world seems to know nothing of it save the name. It is a world without a conscience! And how much do we find the Church of Christ a partaker in the world's sins! 'Evil communications corrupt good manners.' It is sad to observe in many saints, amid much zeal and energy and love, the lack of a tender conscience. For this God is smiting us, and will smite us yet more heavily until He has made it thoroughly tender and sensitive all over, 'hating even the garments spotted by the flesh.' This training of the conscience is a thing of far greater moment than many deem it. God will not rest till He has wrought it. And if the saints will continue to overlook it, if they will not set themselves in good earnest to ask for it, and to strive against everything that would tend to produce searedness and insensibility, they may yet expect some of the sharpest strokes that the hand of God has ever yet administered.

Such, then, is the family discipline! We have seen it as it comes forth from God, and we have seen it as it operates upon man. And is it not all well? What is there about it that should disquiet us, or call forth one murmur either of the lip or heart? That which opens up to us so much more of God and lets us more fully into the secrets of His heart must be blessed, however hard to bear. That which discovers to us the evils within ourselves, which makes us teachable and wise, which gives to the stiff will, flexibility and obedience, which teaches the cold heart to love and expands each straitened affection, which melts the callous conscience into tender sensitiveness, which trains up the whole soul for the glorious kingdom – that must be precious indeed.

Besides, it is the Father's will; and is not this enough for the trustful child? Is not chastisement just one of the methods by which He intimates to us what He would have us to be? Is not *His* way of leading us to the kingdom the safest, surest, shortest way? It is still the paternal hand that is guiding us. What though in seeking to lift us up to a higher level, it has to lay hold of us with a firmer, or it may be a rougher grasp? It is still the paternal voice 'that speaketh unto us as unto children' – dear children – only in a louder, sharper tone to constrain the obedience of His too reluctant sons.

One remark more would I add to these concerning this family discipline. It is not designed even for a moment to separate them and their God, or to overshadow their souls with one suspicion of their Father's heart. That it has done so at times, I know; but that it ought never to do so I am most firmly persuaded. Is it not one of the tests of sonship, and shall that, without which we are not accounted sons, make us doubt our sonship, or suspect the love of our God? That love claims at all times, whether in sorrow or in joy, our simple, fullhearted, peaceful confidence. It is at all times the same, and chastisement is but a more earnest expression of its infinite sincerity and depth. Let us do justice to it, and to Him out of whom it flows. Let us not give it the unworthy treatment which it too often receives at our thankless hands. Let us beware of 'falling from grace' at the very time when God is coming down to us to spread out before us more largely than before all the treasures of His grace. 'We have known and believed the love that God hath to us,' is to be our song. It ought always to be the family song! And shall it cease or sink low at the very time when it ought to be loudest and strongest? Should not trial just draw from us the apostle's triumphant boast: 'Who shall separate us from the love of Christ? Shall tribulation, or distress, or persecution, or famine, or nakedness, or peril, or sword? ... Nay, in all these things we are more than conquerors through him that loved us. For I am persuaded that neither death, nor life, nor angels, nor principalities, nor powers, nor things present, nor things to come, nor height, nor depth, nor any other creature, shall be able to separate us from the love of God, which is in

Christ Jesus our Lord' (Rom. 8:35-39). For is it not just when we are brought under chastening that we enter upon the realities of consolation, the certainties of love, and the joys of heavenly fellowship in ways unknown and unimagined before?

# 5

# THE FAMILY RODS

We hear of the 'rod of the wicked,' and we are told that it 'shall not rest upon the lot of the righteous' (Ps. 125:3). This may mean that wicked men are God's rod for chastening His people, and that, though permitted to light upon them, it shall not rest or abide upon them, but shall be destroyed, as was the Assyrian, who was used by God as the 'rod of his anger' for afflicting Israel. In this sense it gives us the blessed assurance that the triumph of the wicked over the saints is short, that their devices and oppressions shall last but for a moment, and that the Church's sufferings at their hands shall soon be over. Wicked men may be the sword of God (Ps. 17:13), as was Pilate, when he lifted the sword against the man that was Jehovah's friend, or as Herod was when he beheaded John in prison; but that sword shall soon be broken. A wound now and then it may inflict, but that is all. It neither moves nor smites save when God allows. Nor does it come, save with a blessing on its edge. 'They mean it not so,' yet God means it, and that is enough for us. He makes the wrath of man to praise Him. 'There shall no evil happen to the just; when he shall hear of evil tidings he shall not be afraid.'

But the 'rod of the wicked' may mean that rod with which He smites the wicked in His fierce anger. In this sense there is no rod for the righteous. Such a rod never either lights upon them nor rests upon them. Their rod is not the rod of the wicked. It is the family rod. They have done with wrath. Over them no curse can ever rest. 'There is no condemnation to them that are in Christ Jesus.' The rod may *seem* to speak of frowns and anger, but it is only a seeming; there is not a glance of vengeance in the Chastener's eye. It is a correcting rod, but not a destroying one. Its object is not to punish but to chasten; not to injure but to bless. 'God distributeth sorrows in his anger' (Job 21:17), but these are not for His saints.

God has, however, not *one* rod for His children, but many. For each child He has a peculiar rod, and at different times He uses different rods. It will be profitable for us to consider what those are, and how they are applied.

*1. Bodily sickness.* The body operates very powerfully upon the soul both for good and for evil. In what way or to what extent we cannot tell. Nor do I wish to discuss this question at all. But, knowing how the soul is acted on by the body, I cannot help think that one of God's designs in sickness is to operate upon the soul through the body. We are not conscious of this; we cannot analyse the process; the effects are hidden from view. Yet it does seem as if sickness of body were made to contribute directly to the health of the soul in some way or other known only to God. Hence, the apostle speaks of delivering 'such an one unto Satan for the destruction of the flesh, that the spirit may be saved in the day of the Lord Jesus' (1 Cor. 5:5). On this point, however, I do not dwell; only it would be well for us to consider whether God is not by this intimating to us the exceeding danger of pampering the flesh; for the weakening of the flesh does help forward the strengthening of the spirit; and the mortifying of our members which are upon the earth – the crucifying the flesh with its affections and lusts – does tend to quicken and invigorate the soul. Apart from this, however, there are other things to be kept in view.

Sickness prostrates us. It cuts into the very centre of our carnal nature; it exposes in all their deformity 'the lust of the flesh, the lust of the eye, and the pride of life'. What vanity is seen in these upon a sickbed! These are our three idols; and these, sickness dashes down into the dust.

Sickness takes us aside and sets us alone with God. We are taken into His private chamber, and there He converses with us face to face. The world is far off, our relish for it is gone, and we are alone with *God*. Many are the words of grace and truth which He then speaks to us. All our former props are struck away, and we must now lean on God alone. The things of earth are felt to be vanity; man's help useless. Man's praise and man's sympathy desert us; we are cast wholly upon God that we may learn that His praise and His sympathy are enough. 'If it were not for pain,' says one, 'I should spend less time with God. If I had not been kept awake with pain, I should have lost one of the sweetest experiences I ever had in my life. The disorder of my body is the very help I want from God; and if it does its work before it lays me in the dust, it will raise me up to Heaven.' It was thus that Job was 'chastened upon his bed with pain, and the multitude of his bones with strong pain,' that after being tried he might 'come forth as gold' (Job 23:10).

Sickness teaches that activity of service is not the only way in which God is glorified. 'They also serve who only stand and wait.' Active duty is that which man judges most acceptable; but God shows us that in bearing and suffering He is also glorified. Perhaps we were pursuing a path of our own and required to be arrested. Perhaps we were too much harassed by a bustling world and needed retirement, yet could find no way of obtaining it till God laid us down, and drew us aside into a desert place, because of the multitude pressing upon us.

No one of the family rods is more in use than

this, sometimes falling lightly on us, at other times more heavily. Let us kiss the rod. Let us open our mouth wide to the blessing, seeking so to profit by each bodily ailment, slight or severe, that it may bring forth in us the peaceable fruits of righteousness. 'I know,' says one, 'of no greater blessing than health, except pain and sickness.'

*2. Bereavement.* This is the bitterest of all earthly sorrows. It is the sharpest arrow in the quiver of God. To love tenderly and deeply and then to part; to meet together for the last time on earth; to bid farewell for time; to have all past remembrances of home and kindred broken up – this is the reality of sorrow. To look upon that face that shall smile on us no more; to press those lips that shall speak to us no more; to stand by the cold side of father, mother, brother, sister, friend, yet hear no sound and receive no greeting; to carry to the tomb the beloved of our hearts, and then to return to a desolate home with a blank in one region of our souls, which shall never again be filled till Jesus come with all His saints; this is the bitterness of grief; this is the wormwood and the gall!

It is this rod which ever and anon God is laying upon us. Nor is there any that we need more than this. By it He is making room for Himself in hearts that had been filled with other objects and engrossed with other loves. He is jealous of our affection, for He claims it all as His own; and every idol He will utterly abolish. For our sakes as well as for His own He can suffer no rival in the heart. Perhaps the joys of an earthly home are stealing away our hearts from the many mansions above. God breaks in upon us in mercy and turns that home into a wilderness. Our sin finds us out; we mourn over it and seek anew to realize our heavenly citizenship and set out anew upon our pilgrim way, alone and yet not alone, for the Father is with us. Perhaps we are sitting 'at ease in Zion', comfortable and contented, amid the afflictions of a suffering Church and the miseries of a world that owns no Saviour and fears no God. Jehovah speaks and we awake. He takes to Himself some happy saint, or smites to the dust some wretched sinner. We are troubled at the stroke. We mourn our lethargy. While we slept, a fellow-sinner has gone down to be with the devil and his angels. The death of the one stirs us up; the death of the other solemnizes and overawes us.

Thus as saint after saint ascends to God, we begin to feel that Heaven is far more truly the family home than earth. We have far more brethren above than we have below. And each bereavement reminds us of this. It reminds us, too, that the coming of the Lord draweth nigh, and makes us look out more wistfully from our eastern casement for the first streaks of the rising dawn. It kindles in us strong desires for the day of happy meeting in our Father's house, when we shall clasp inseparable hands and climb in company the everlasting hills. Meanwhile it bids us give our hearts to Jesus only. It does for us what the departure of the two strangers from Heaven did to the disciples on the Mount of Transfiguration – it leaves us alone with Jesus. It turns into deep experience that longing for home contained in the apostle's words, 'having a desire to depart and to be with Christ which is far better.'

The more that bereavement transforms earth into a desert, the more are our desires drawn up to Heaven. Our treasures having been transferred to Heaven, our hearts must follow them. Earth's hopes are smitten and we are taught to look for 'that blessed hope, the glorious appearing of the great God and our Saviour Jesus Christ'. The night is falling and the flowers are folding up; but as they do so they bid us look upward and see star after star appearing upon the darkening sky.

3. *Adversity.* This may be the loss of substance, or it may be the loss of our good name, or it may be the falling away of friends, or it may be the wrath of enemies, or it may be the disappointment of our hopes: these are what is meant by adversity. But let Job tell us what it means. 'Behold, he breaketh down, and it cannot be built again, he shutteth up a man, and there can be no opening' (Job 12:14). 'He hath made me weary: thou hast

made desolate all my company ... I was at ease, but he hath broken me asunder: he hath also taken me by the neck, and shaken me to pieces, and set me up for his mark. His archers compass me round about, he cleaveth my reins asunder, and doth not spare.... He breaketh me with breach upon breach, he runneth upon me like a giant .... My face is foul with weeping, and on my eyelids is the shadow of death' (Job 16:7, 12, 13, 14, 16). 'My days are past, my purposes are broken off, even the thoughts of my heart' (Job 17:11). 'He hath fenced up my way that I cannot pass, and he hath set darkness in my paths. He hath stripped me of my glory and taken the crown from my head. He hath destroyed me on every side, and I am gone: and mine hope hath he removed like a tree.... He hath put my brethren far from me, and mine acquaintance are verily estranged from me' (Job 19:8-10, 13). These are some of the drops in the bitter cup of adversity that was given to that patient saint to drink. And they are recorded for our use, on whom the ends of the world have come, and to whom these last days may perhaps fill a cup as bitter and protracted as his.

Yet let us count it all joy when we fall into divers tribulations, knowing this, that the trying of our faith worketh patience; but 'let patience have her perfect work, that ye may be perfect and entire, wanting nothing' (James 1:2-4). We are cast into poverty, but how can we be poor so long as Christ is rich; and is not this poverty sent to make us prize His unsearchable riches and to buy of Him the gold tried in the fire that we may be rich? Our good name is lost through slander and false accusation. The finger of public scorn is perhaps pointed at us, and wicked men are exalted over us triumphing in our reproach. Yet have we not the approving eye of God, and is it not enough if He still honours us and knows our innocence? Let our good name go if God sees fit thus to humble us. We have the 'white stone, and in the stone a new name written, which no man knoweth save he that receiveth it' (Rev. 2:17).

Friends fall off and enemies arise: false brethren turn against us, and we are doomed to bear the revilings and persecutions of those whom we have never wronged but ever love. But the friendship of Jesus is still ours. No earthly disaster or persecutor can ever rob us of that. Nay, the coldness of those we counted on as tried and true only draws us the closer to Him, the warmth of whose love knows no abatement nor end. Joseph passed thoroughly this trial, and the Lord set him upon Pharaoh's throne. Moses passed through it and became 'king in Jeshurun'. Job passed through it and was exalted with double honour. Let us 'take … the prophets who have spoken in the name of the Lord, for an example of suffering affliction, and of patience. Behold, we count them happy which endure. Ye have heard of the

71

patience of Job, and have seen the end of the Lord; that the Lord is very pitiful, and of tender mercy' (James 5:10-11).

Oftentimes nothing but adversity will do for us. 'I spake unto thee in thy prosperity; but thou saidst, I will not hear. This hath been thy manner from thy youth, that thou obeyedst not my voice' (Jer. 22:21). We need to be turned out of a home on earth that we may seek a home in Heaven. Earth's music is too seducing and takes away our relish for the new song. God must either hush it or take us apart into a desert place that we may no longer be led captive by it but may have our ear open only to the heavenly melody. We cannot be trusted with too full a cup, or too pleasant a resting place. We abuse everything that God has given us, and prove ourselves not trustworthy as to any one of them. Some God cannot trust with health; they need sickness to keep them low and make them walk softly all their days. They need spare diet, lest the flesh should get the mastery. Others He cannot trust with prosperity; they need adversity to humble them, lest, like Jeshurun, they should wax 'fat and kick'. Others He cannot trust with riches; they must be kept poor, lest covetousness should spring up and pierce them through with many sorrows. Others He cannot trust with friends; they make idols of them, they give their hearts to them; and this interferes with the claims of Jehovah to have us altogether as His own.

But still in all this God dealeth with us as with the members of His own family. Never for a moment does He lose sight of this. Neither should we. So that when these things overtake us, when we are thus 'judged,' we should feel that we are 'chastened of the Lord, that we should not be condemned with the world'; we should learn not merely to *submit* to the rod, but to kiss and welcome it, not merely to acquiesce in chastisement, but to 'glory in tribulation, knowing that tribulation worketh patience, and patience experience, and experience hope, and hope maketh not ashamed'. We should learn not merely to praise God *in* affliction, but to praise Him *for* it. We should see that the lot of the afflicted is far more enviable than that of him who is 'let alone'; and, instead of trembling when we see the dark cloud of sorrow coming over us, we should tremble far more when we see it passing off, lest, perchance, that which came charged with blessing to us, should, through our stout-heartedness and unteachableness, leave us callous and unblessed.

# 6

## THE TYPES

The ordinance in Israel concerning the meat-offering of the first fruits was of a very peculiar kind. Thus it was commanded, 'If thou offer a meat-offering of thy firstfruits unto the LORD, thou shalt offer for the meat-offering of thy first fruits, green ears of corn dried by the fire' (Lev. 2:14).

Christ is, we know, pre-eminently the firstfruits. It is He, then, who is specially prefigured by these green ears of corn dried by the fire. In this 'corn' we discern the type of one who belongs to earth, partaker of our very nature. It springs up in our fields, it is nourished by our soil, it is watered by our showers, it is ripened by our sun. So was it with Jesus. He was truly Man, one of us, 'the Word made flesh,' the Man who 'drank of the brook by the way.'

The corn was to be plucked when green and then dried by the fire, not in the ordinary gradual way by the heat of the sun. It was to be prematurely ripened by what we would call unnatural means, the exposure to artificial heat. In this also we see Jesus, the Man of sorrows, subjected to the Father's wrath, the wrath of Him who is a consuming fire, and withered into ripeness before His time. He did not come to His grave 'in a full age, like a shock of corn in its season' (Job 5:26). He did not grow up to manhood in the calm, refreshing sunshine of Jehovah's smile. He was scorched with fiery heat, within and without, till age appeared upon His much-marred visage, while as yet the greenness of His strength was upon Him, so that the Jews, looking upon His wasted form, spoke of Him as one who had well-nigh reached His fiftieth year (John 8:57).

Such is the view He gives of Himself in the Book of Psalms. In these we at once recognize the 'green ears of corn dried by the fire'. For thus He speaks, 'My strength is dried up like a potsherd; and my tongue cleaveth to my jaws; and thou hast brought me unto the dust of death' (Ps. 22:15). Again, He says, 'Mine eye is consumed with grief, yea, my soul and my belly; for my life is spent with grief, and my years with sighing: my strength faileth .... my bones are consumed' (Ps. 31:9f.). Again, we hear Him saying, 'Mine eye is consumed because of grief; it waxeth old because of all mine enemies' (Ps. 6:7). Such, then, was Jesus: withered and dried up before His time by reason of the sorrow which He endured for us.

But these green ears dried up by the fire are no less a description of the saints than of their Lord. Certainly they apply to Him in a way such as they never can apply to us. Yet they do stand forth as a type of the whole Church, who are also called like Jesus, 'the firstfruits'. All the members of His body from the beginning have been just such as these dried ears of green corn. Hear, for instance, one of them speaking, 'I am like a bottle in the smoke'; or again, 'My bones waxed old through my roaring all the day long .... my moisture is turned into the drought of summer' (Ps. 32:3-4).

By such an emblem as this was the Church's career of tribulation set before Israel. And it is most interesting for us to look at our trials in the light of so expressive a figure. Their object is to *ripen* us: it may be before the time; it may be in a way such as the flesh shrinks from; but still their object is to ripen us. The sorrows that compass us about are all ripening our graces, as well as withering out of us the green, rank, unripe luxuriance of earth. The heat may be great, but it shall not consume us; it will only make the ripening process a speedier one. It will shorten the way to perfect holiness and eternal glory; and shall we shrink from that which makes the process shorter?

But there was another ordinance in Israel setting forth the tribulation of the Church. The mercy seat and the cherubim were to be both made of pure gold, 'of beaten work' (Exod. 25:17-18). Now, as the cherubim were doubtless the symbols of redeemed men, the Church of Christ, this type is very striking. Both the mercy seat and the cherubim were to be of one piece, for 'both he who sanctifieth and they who are sanctified are all of one'. They are of pure gold, and this denotes their exceeding preciousness. They are made of 'beaten gold', to intimate the process through which they both had passed. The mercy seat was fashioned into shape and made after the pattern showed in the mount by the stroke of the hammer. So Jesus was 'made perfect through suffering'. In like manner the cherubim were to be beaten into the intended shape and model. So with the saints. It is through this process that they must pass, and it is thus they are brought into that perfect shape which God has designed for them.

What, then, is the process through which the saints are passing now but just this? They are now under the manner of the Spirit, that by this they may be fashioned into the likeness of cherubim, which in the Book of Revelation are set before us as the upbearers of Jehovah's throne and glory, as well as the inheritors thereof. And what is all the 'beating' to which we may be subjected when compared with the glory for which it is preparing us?

There is another figure used by our Lord in speaking of His Church. He compares her to an injured, afflicted, friendless widow. Widowhood, then, is properly the Church's condition here. And this is her grief. Her Lord is absent, and His absence is one of her bitterest trials. It forms one long-continued sorrow. It makes such a blank on earth that we feel as if this of itself were grief enough, even were there none besides. And were the Church to realize fully her estate of widowhood, until the Lord come, she would find in this, no doubt, a new grief to which she was blind before, but a grief which operates with most blessed efficacy in sanctifying her and in keeping her apart from the *world*.

She is a stranger in a land of strangers. She is lonely and unfriended, sitting apart from earthly joy and fellowship. He whom she loves is far away. This separation is, as a saint of old expresses it, 'like a mountain of iron upon her heavy heart.' She longs to be with Him. She sighs for the day of meeting. And all this though sad is both sanctifying and solemnizing. It is a daily burden, a continual chastening, yet it is well. It loosens from earth. It lifts up to Heaven. It makes the world less fascinating. It prepares for the inseparable union: the meeting time – the bridal day.

There are other figures given us of the suffering Church. But let these suffice. They will help us to understand our true condition and to expect nothing else than tribulation here. No strange thing is happening to us. It is no strange thing that the green ears of corn should be dried with fire. It is no strange thing that the cherubim should be made of beaten gold. It is no strange thing that, in the absence of the Bridegroom, the bride should mourn.

# 7

## THE PROVING

There are no beings about whom we make so many mistakes as our own selves. 'The heart is deceitful above all things,' and besides this, the 'deceitfulness of sin' is unsearchable. So that when the deceitfulness of our heart and the deceitfulness of sin come together, we need not wonder that the effect should be ignorance of ourselves.

Besides, we are unwilling to search. We shrink from the exposure which such a scrutiny would make. No doubt the consciousness of being forgiven takes away much of this reluctance. We are not so unwilling to know the worst when we are assured that however hideous the pollution thus dragged to light, it can never come between us and God. For with God all is peace. The blood that sprinkles us has made it a simple impossibility for God ever to be angry with us again. So that we come to realize in some degree the blessedness of the man whose transgression is forgiven; our spirit is without guile. We have no object now in concealing anything from God or ourselves. We become open, frank, straightforward. Still the search is a painful one, and we would rather postpone it. It might bring many things to light which would shock and humble us. It might alarm us with the extent of the evil which still remains in us, even though it could not bring us into condemnation. Hence, we are slow to learn, or even to inquire into, the evil that cleaves to us still.

Moreover, we are not at all persuaded that there is so very much evil in us. We do not know ourselves. Our convictions of sin have been but shallow, and we are beginning to imagine that the conflict between the flesh and the spirit is not so very fierce and deadly as we had conceived it to be. We think we have rid ourselves of many of our sins entirely, and are in a fair way speedily getting rid of all the rest. The depths of sin in us we have never sounded; the number of our abominations we have never thought of marking. We have been sailing smoothly to the kingdom, and perhaps at times were wondering how our lot should be so different from the saints of old. We thought, too, that we had overcome many of our corruptions. The old man was crucified. It seemed dead, or at least feigned itself to be so in order to deceive us. Our lusts had abated. Our tempers had improved. Our souls were calm and equable. Our mountains stood strong, and we were saying, 'We shall never be moved.' The victory over self and sin seemed, in some measure, won. Alas, we were blind! We were profoundly ignorant of our hearts.

Well, the trial came. It swept *over* us like a cloud of the night, or rather *through* us like an icy blast, piercing and chilling us to the vitals. Then the old man within us awoke, and, as if in response to the uproar without, a fiercer tempest broke loose within. We felt as if the four winds of Heaven had been let loose to strive together upon the great deep within us. Unbelief arose in its former strength. Rebelliousness raged in every region of our soul. Unsubdued passions resumed their strength. We were utterly dismayed at the fearful scene. But yesterday this seemed impossible. Alas, we knew not the strength of sin nor the evil of our hearts till God thus allowed them to break loose.

It was thus He dealt with Israel; and for this end He led them into the desert. 'The LORD thy God led thee these forty years in the wilderness, to humble thee, and to prove thee, to know what was in thine heart' (Deut. 8:2). Their desert trials put them to the proof. And when thus proved, what iniquity was found in them! What sin came out which had lain hidden and unknown before! The trial did not create the evil: it merely brought out what was there already, unnoticed and unfelt, like a torpid adder. Then the heart's deep fountains were broken up, and streams of pollution came rushing out, black as Hell.

Rebellion, unbelief, fretfulness, atheism, idolatry, self-will, self-confidence, self-pleasing – all burst out when the blast of the desert met them in the face and called Egypt to remembrance with its luxurious plenty. Thus they were proved.

Even so it is with the saints still. God chastens them that He may draw forth the evil that is lying concealed and unsuspected within. The rod smites us on the tenderest part, and we start up in a moment as if in arms against God. The flesh, the old man, is cut to the quick, and forthwith arouses itself, displaying all of a sudden much of its former strength. When it was asleep we did not know its power, but now that it has been awakened, its remains of strength appal us.

It is not till the sea is 'troubled,' that 'its waters cast up mire and dirt'. When all was calm, there seemed naught but purity pervading it, and ripple folded over ripple in the still brightness of its transparent green. But the winds break loose, the tempest stirs its lowest depths, and then all is changed. Thus we see it in the saints. When calamity breaks over them like a tempest, then the hidden evils of their hearts awaken. Sins scarcely known before display themselves. The heart pours out its wickedness. Hard thoughts of God arise. Atheistical murmurings break out and refuse to be restrained.

Questionings both of His wisdom and of His love are muttered; yea, how often do they assume a more explicit form, and we ask, 'If God be so loving and wise, why is it thus?' We could not have expected such treatment at His hands. Distrust and unbelief assume the mastery, and we refuse to acquiesce to His will. It seems hard to be smitten so severely and laid so low. For a while it seems as if the heart were determined to think evil thoughts of God and never to think well of Him again. And, though a calm ensues and we become both ashamed and terrified at our rebelliousness, still the heart has given forth its pollution. We have learned its unsearchable depths of evil. We are led, on the one hand, into deeper views of our own amazing and incredible vileness; and on the other, into fuller discoveries of the abounding grace of God. We learn to prize more the open fountain, and we betake ourselves anew for covering to the righteousness of the Righteous One.

It is remarkable that when the saints of old were tried and proved, there was found in them not only evil but the very evil we should least of all have anticipated. We should have said of Noah, for instance, that he was one whose sobriety and self-restraint would be carried with him to his grave. He stood alone amid a luxurious, sensual, intoxicated world, condemning their lasciviousness and revelry. Yet no sooner is he placed in circumstances of temptation than he falls. Noah becomes drunken!

Again, Abraham stands out preeminent for faith and courage; yet, when he goes to Egypt and Gerar, his faith gives way, and he utters lies through fear. Lot had withstood all the sensuality and filthiness of Sodom, and his righteous soul mourned over their abominations; yet, scarce is he delivered from the city's destruction than he falls into drunkenness and lust equal to that of the cities that had been consumed. Job, though marked for his patience, gave way to impatience in the day of trial. Moses, the meekest of all men, displayed his anger and 'spake unadvisedly with his lips'. David was one of the bravest that ever fought the battles of the Lord in Israel, and he had gone out against Goliath with a sling and a stone, yet when he fled before Saul and came to King Achish at Gath his courage was gone, and he feigned himself a madman through fear of his enemies. Elijah had stood before kings without trembling to pronounce the sentence of judgment, to shut up the heavens, and to wield the sword of Jehovah's vengeance, though alone amid tens of thousands. Yet he flees before a woman's threat, he gives up all for lost and requests to die.

Ezekiel, whose character shines out as one of singular holiness and obedience, yet records against himself a strange instance of unsubmissiveness, when sent by God on an errand of judgment to Israel: 'I went in bitterness, in the heat [or, hot anger] of my spirit; but the hand of the LORD was strong upon me' (Ezek. 3:14). Peter's attachment to his Lord is one of his peculiar characteristics, yet it was Peter who denied Him. John was the disciple who seems to have been most like his Master in gentleness and love, yet it was John who wanted to call down fire from Heaven upon the Samaritan village.

Lord, what is man! And what is a human heart – the heart even of thy saints when proved and held up to view? 'O heart, heart,' said John Berridge of himself, 'what art thou? A mass of fooleries and absurdities, the vainest, wickedest, craftiest, foolishest thing in nature.' What deep-hidden evil, what selfishness, what pride, what harsh tempers, what worldliness come out in a moment, when the stroke goes deep into the soul! How long Job remained steadfast, holding fast his integrity and confidence in God! Stroke after stroke laid him prostrate, yet he gave glory to God in the midst of desolation and sorrow. The inner circle of *self* had not been reached. But his friends rose up against him and addressed him as a man marked out by God as guilty then his faith and patience gave way. The very centre of his being had been reached and probed; and forth came the stream of impatience and unbelief. It takes a sharp arrow and a strongly drawn bow to pierce into the inmost circle; yet God in kindness spares not. The seat of the disease must be reached, and its real nature brought out to the light.

Of all the evils which are thus drawn forth from the heart of the saint, the worst, and yet the commonest, are hard thoughts of God. Yet who would have expected this? Once, indeed, in our unbelieving days our souls were full of these. Our thoughts of God were all evil together. When the Holy Spirit wrought in our hearts the mighty change, the special thing which He accomplished was teaching us to think well of God, showing us how little He had deserved these hard thoughts from us, how much He had deserved the opposite. The wondrous tale of manifold love, which the gospel brought to us, won our hearts and made us ashamed of our distrust. We said then, Surely we shall never think ill of God again. 'Though he slay me, yet will I trust in him.' We thought that affliction would only make us cleave to Him the more. Yet scarcely does He begin to smite us than our former thoughts return. We wonder why He should treat us thus. We suspect His love and faithfulness. Our hold of His grace seems to loosen, as if at times it would wholly give way.

We are like Jonah with his withered gourd. We think we do well to be angry even unto death. God does not seem the same loving God as when first we believed and tasted forgiveness from His gracious hands. Alas, the treachery of our hearts has been at length discovered. We find that we were not serving God for naught.

May He not expostulate with us and ask us,

'Doest thou well to be angry?' Would not this question close our lips forever? Doest thou well to be angry or desponding, when God hath forgiven all thine iniquities and removed them from thee, as far as the East is from the West? Doest thou well to be angry when thou art delivered from the wrath to come, as well as from a present evil world, and safely lodged within the clefts of the rock with Jesus as thy companion there? Doest thou well to be angry when the Father's love is thine assured portion and the kingdom of the Son thine inheritance forever? Doest thou well to be angry when the night is far spent and the day is at hand, when the distant eastern clouds are taking on their rosy fringes, and the daystar is preparing to arise?[1]

---

1. God's chastened ones will find many precious words of counsel and consolation in Samuel Rutherford's letters. Having been tried, he knew how to speak a word in season to the weary. Hear some of them, 'I wonder many times that ever a child of God should have a sad heart, considering what the Lord is preparing for him.' 'When we shall come home, and enter into the possession of our brother's fair kingdom, and when our heads shall find the weight of the eternal crown of glory, and when we shall look back to pains and sufferings, then shall we see life and sorrow to be less than one step or stride from a prison to a glory, and that our little inch of time-suffering is not worthy of our first night's welcome home to heaven.' 'However matters go, the worst shall be a tired traveller, and a joyful and sweet welcome home.'

# 8

# THE REBUKING

It is worthwhile noticing the word which is used in the two well-known passages which speak of chastisement, 'Nor faint when thou art *rebuked* of him' (Heb. 12:5). 'As many as I love, I *rebuke* and chasten' (Rev. 3:19). A little inquiry into its meaning and a little comparing of texts will help to set it in its true light.

It is the same word used in Matthew 18:15: 'If thy brother shall trespass against thee, go and *tell him his fault.*' It is the same word used in Luke 3:19, when John is said to have *reproved* Herod. It is the same word used in John 16:8: 'When he is come, he will *reprove* the world of sin.' We learn, then, from these expressions, that rebuke is not simply some stern word or frown, implying displeasure on the part of God, but such a frown which 'tells us our faults' – such a frown which reproves or convicts us of sin. It is God's way of pointing out what He sees to be amiss in us, of calling our attention to it as a thing which displeases Him, and, on account of which, if not put away, He must certainly deal with us in chastisement.

The word *rebuke* seems to imply something more gentle than chastisement. And it is of some importance to consider it in this light. I know not a better illustration of it than Christ's addresses to the churches of Asia. The especial preciousness of these lies in this, that they show us what the heart of Christ is when reproving. What a discovery do they give us of this! Let us hear Him addressing them. Thus He rebukes the angel of the church of Ephesus: 'Nevertheless I have somewhat against thee, because thou hast left thy first love; remember therefore from whence thou art fallen, and repent.' Thus He rebukes the church of Pergamos: 'I have a few things against thee, because thou hast there them that hold the doctrine of Balaam … repent, or else I will come unto thee quickly, and will fight against thee with the sword of my mouth.' In like manner we might quote His other rebukes to the other churches as illustrations of our meaning. But these are enough. They show the gentleness of the reprover both in the manner and the language. They are faithful, indeed, but how delicate, how tender, how mild! They point out what is amiss with all distinctness and directness, yet in a manner the most fitted to win and in language the least likely to offend. He begins each of them by making most gracious mention of the past services and excellent deeds of the angel of the church, as if desirous to show how willing He was to praise, insofar as He could, and how unwilling to blame, save when it could not be avoided. In listening to this voice speaking from Heaven, we seem to hear that same meek and lowly One that once spake on earth in the house of Simon the Pharisee. Wishing to reprove him for his evil thoughts of the woman who stood behind the Lord and washed His feet with her tears, He began thus mildly His rebuke, 'Simon, I have somewhat to say unto thee.'

Yet while the rebuke of God is thus mild and loving, it is both faithful and solemn. It is faithful, for it hides nothing from us. Its tone is soft, yet the words are full of meaning. They are quite explicit in their condemnation of the sin perceived in us. And the rebuke of Jehovah is a solemn thing. It is not the rebuke of wrath, for that has passed away, yet it makes us stand in awe. The rebuke of love is as solemn a thing as the rebuke of wrath. A parent's rebuke is much to a loving child, how much more is the rebuke of our God – the God who made Heaven and earth!

Many are the rebukes which He administers. Some of them are lighter and others heavier. Yet in both He is laying His finger upon sin and intimating distinctly His desire that we should turn from it. To the former kind I fear we oftentimes give but little heed. The touch of transient pain, a brief illness, a slight indisposition, a passing weakness, some common domestic vexation, some trivial casualty, some few days parting from one we love, some unkind word where least we looked for it, some disappointment or annoyance – these are all fatherly rebukes of the lighter and gentler kind. They are not so sharp as many others, yet they are not the less on that account the indications of a father's will. They are apt to be overlooked, for they are slighter and commoner then many and do not force themselves upon our notice. Yet surely it is worth our while to point them out and to make them the subject of special and prolonged consideration.

It is difficult to understand why we should so much undervalue them. To one who weighs them aright, they cannot but seem peculiarly precious and affecting. Their frequency makes us familiar with them, and on this account we slight them. Sad and strange! Does not their frequency show the unwearied pains that God is taking with us, giving us precept upon precept, line upon line? Should that very thing in them which displays God's untiring earnestness, His assiduous vigilance, and intense anxiety for our welfare tempt us to disregard such dealings? Their mildness, also, as well as their frequency tends to make us undervalue them. Unaccountable perversity! They are so slight and so gentle; therefore, they are not to be owned as the laying on of a father's hand! Had they been sharper and heavier they would have been recognized as such, but being so tender they are hardly worthy of our serious notice!

On this point I am persuaded that an admonition is much needed, not merely by a heedless world, but even by the saints of God. The point adverted to is a much neglected one, and yet it is one which every day's events press upon our notice. A raging fever prostrates us. Our strength gives way. Our life is despaired of. Then we say, 'This is the finger of God. This is His rebuke.' But we take a slight cold, or sustain some slight injury – there is no danger and perhaps no piercing pain, O then, alas! we do not own the doing of God; or, at the most, we own it vaguely and carelessly. The gentleness of the infliction makes us feel at liberty to undervalue it, and to forget it as coming from God. Ah! it is thus that we 'despise his chastenings'.

And what is the consequence? We draw upon ourselves severer chastisement. We provoke God to visit us with heavier blows. We compel Him to chastise by our heedlessness of His rebuke. We make bitter trial absolutely necessary.

Let us never forget this. It is our own forwardness and negligence that impose a necessity for the infliction of suffering. Affliction is not a desirable thing in itself. It would be better could it be avoided. God afflicts not willingly. But we constrain Him. Many a sorrow we might escape were we not so heedless and unbelieving.

Most slowly and reluctantly does God stretch out His hand to chasten. For a while He would most slightly and mildly. If we may speak after the manner of men, He just hints or whispers His reproof. He is most unwilling to employ sharpness. He tarries long. He lingers on His way to smite. He tries other means. He sends milder trials first that we may be led to self-searching and repentance and that He may be spared the necessity of inflicting a heavier blow. But we trifle with these; and then, at last, He lifts up His voice and speaks in a way which can neither be overlooked nor mistaken. How sad that we should thus so stubbornly persist in filling the cup of sorrow which God would fain have spared us!

Let us open our ears to the rebuke of God. His 'still small voice' should be as effectual as the lightning or the earthquake. Let us learn the meaning and use of slighter trials. Let us count no touch of pain or grief, however mild or transient, too insignificant for our most serious thought. This would save us much. It would teach us many a blessed lesson in an easy, pleasant way. Every trouble, however light, comes fragrant with blessing. Shall we then overlook it or thrust it away? It is a new opportunity of getting nearer God and learning more of His love. How foolish, how sinful, to disregard it! God is saying to us, 'Improve this light cross, and you will not need a heavier.' But we are deaf. And, oh, how much this deafness costs us!

It is not, however, our deafness under light troubles only that draws on us the heavier. We are too heedless even of these heavier ones, and this prepares for us heavier still. The easy way in which some get over trials is very sad. There is a vehement outburst of feeling at the moment; and occasionally there may be a recurrence of this for some time after the calamity has spent itself, but, with the exception of such fits of grief, there is nothing like laying the trial to heart. To lay a visitation solemnly to heart is something very different from indulging in wild bursts of grief. Hence, it will generally be found that those who give way to these are often, during the intervals between them, very easy and mirthful. This unequal pressure of trial is not only in itself injurious to the soul, but it neutralizes the right influence of trial, and thus renders necessary another and more stunning blow.

Hence, it is that we so often observe that when God takes up a case in earnest, if anyone may so speak, it is either by a succession of strokes, following each other closely, or else by a long protracted sorrow. And it is we who procure these things unto ourselves in that we have forsaken the Lord our God, whom He led by the way (Jer. 2:17). Billow after billow breaks over us, but we ourselves have called forth the storm; and it is our perversity that is keeping it alive, nay, perhaps, raising the surges higher till we are well-nigh overwhelmed. Had we but yielded to God at once, and allowed Him to bless us as He desired, one wave might have been enough, and ere evening the storm breeze might have died away.

Yet, even in this there is consolation. Our foolishness is making our voyage a rough one, but it is homeward bound. All these many blasts and billows are toward Canaan, not away from it; and sometimes, from their topmost crest, we get a brighter glimpse of our eternal heritage than from the level calm of more unruffled days. It brightens the blackness of the tempest, and disarms it of many a terror to know that each blast, however fierce, is bearing us homeward, that each billow, however rough, is carrying us more swiftly to our desired haven.

# 9

# THE PURIFYING

Chastisement supposes *sin.* Suffering does not, for Jesus suffered, nay, 'learned obedience by the things which he suffered.' But chastisement does. Some have, indeed, applied the word chastisement to Jesus also, for He was 'made perfect through suffering'. And in the sense of passing through discipline that He might know by experience our condition here and be seen as the doer of the Father's will, the Man that 'pleased not himself' – in this sense His sorrows might be called by that name. Yet in no other. For although tempted in all points like as we are, He was without sin. But in our case it is altogether different. It is sin in us that draws down the infliction, just as the rod attracts the lightning from the clouds.

Yet it is all forgiven sin. In looking to the cross we found forgiveness. As believers in Jesus, we 'have no more conscience of sin'. Still the flesh remains. The old man is ever at work within us. 'Iniquities prevail against us'; and though we know that they are purged away, still they cleave to us. Our nature is still defiled though our conscience has been cleansed. It is against sin still existing within us, though forgiven, that chastisement is directed.

The casting of gold or silver into the furnace implies there is dross upon them that requires to be purged out with fire. Were there no dross, there would be no need for furnace or fire or refiner's labour. These are but means of getting rid of the dross. The fire which the Lord is to kindle in the earth, when He comes again, proves that sin is found upon it. Were there no curse lying on the earth, no purifying fire would be needed. But the blight must be burned out, the trail of the serpent must be swept clean away; and therefore the earth must be cast into the furnace that out of it may come a new and more glorious creation, fit for God to look upon, and for holy men to dwell in, and from which, therefore, every trace of corruption must be totally erased.

So with chastisement. It has reference to sin. Were it not for sin chastisement would be unknown. In Heaven there is no chastisement, for there is no sin. Angels know nothing of it, for they know no sin. They see it afar off. They hear the sad story of earth. They witness the tribulations of the Church but that is all. For it is only where there is sin that there is chastisement. Its existence here is just God's voice, saying, 'I have found iniquity upon the earth.' Its infliction on an individual is God saying, 'I have seen sin on thee.' I do not take up the question as to particular trials being the result of particular sins in individuals. In many cases we know that this is the case. In others it is more doubtful. And hence, though it is well in affliction to ask what special sin or sins God is pointing at, it is wrong in us to fix exclusively upon one or two instead of turning our attention to the whole body of sin and directing our efforts against that.

But chastisement supposes also a determination on the part of God to get rid of sin. It is the expression of His hatred of it, and of His settled purpose to deliver from it. To purify us is what He seeks; and this He is resolved to accomplish at whatever cost. It must be done, for He cannot look upon iniquity. And what is pain if it expel sin? What is sorrow, if it help to purge away the evil of our nature – a lifetime of accumulated dross?

There are several figures which God employs for pointing out His designs in chastising us. Let us enumerate these:

*1. It is a refining.* The saints are 'chosen in the furnace of affliction' (Isa. 48:10), and 'when he hath tried me, I shall come forth as gold' (Job 23:10). The heat of the furnace burns out the dross and leaves the pure metal behind. It is in the furnace that the flesh is destroyed and the old man gets his deathstroke. It is in the furnace that self-confidence is uptorn, unbelief is broken, and faith is strengthened and purified. Were it not for the furnace, what would become of our dross and alloy? And then when the silver is in the crucible, the Refiner Himself comes near. Hear how the Lord hath spoken concerning this: 'Thus saith the LORD of hosts, Behold, I will melt them, and try them; for how shall I do for the daughter of my people?' (Jer. 9:7). 'I will turn my hand upon thee, and purely purge away thy dross, and take away all thy tin' (Isa. 1:25). 'When the Lord ... shall have purged the blood of Jerusalem from the midst thereof by the spirit of judgment, and by the spirit of burning' (Isa. 4:4).

2. *It is a sifting.* 'Lo, I will command, and I will sift the house of Israel among all nations, like as corn is sifted in a sieve' (Amos 9:9). We are God's corn, grown in His fields and gathered in by His hand. Yet we are coarse and rough grain. Many a sifting process we must pass through in order to separate the coarser particles that nothing but the finest may remain. Affliction sifts us. Persecution sifts us. God has many a sieve, some finer and some coarser, and He makes us to pass through them according as we require. He sifts the professing Church, and many fall off. He applies a finer sieve, and many more fall off. He takes each church by itself, each congregation by itself, and sifts them, and many false brethren are discovered. He takes each believer and sifts him individually and his coarser particles pass off. This process is repeated. He is winnowed and

sifted again and again till the grain is purified.

3. *It is a pruning.* 'Every branch that beareth fruit, he purgeth it, that it may bring forth more fruit' (John 15:2). We are the branches of the vine. Christ is the Father's vine: the stem and root of all spiritual life. Over this precious vine the Father watches. His desire is that 'the branch of the Lord should be beautiful and glorious,' that this vine should yield its fruit in its season. Hence, He not only waters it, but keeps it night and day. And He prunes it with the skill and care of a husbandman. He wishes to make each branch fruitful as well as comely, and He spares no pains, for 'herein is he glorified if we bear much fruit'. How much we owe to this heavenly pruning! What rank, luxuriant branches does it cut away! What earthliness, what foolishness, what waywardness, what hastiness, what fleshly lusts, what selfish narrowness are all, one by one, skilfully pruned away by the vinedresser's careful knife!

4. *It is a polishing.* We are 'living stones', placed one by one, upon the great foundation stone laid in Zion for the heavenly temple. These stones must first be quarried out of the mass. This the Holy Spirit does at conversion. Then, when cut out, the hewing and squaring begin. And God uses affliction as His hammer and chisel for accomplishing this. Many a stroke is needed; and after being thus hewn into shape, the polishing

goes on. All roughness must be smoothed away. The stone must be turned around and around on every side that no part of it may be left unpolished.

The temple indeed is above, and we are below. But this is God's design. As the stones of Solomon's temple were all to be prepared at a distance and then brought to Jerusalem, there to be builded together, so the living stones of the heavenly temple are all made ready here to be fitted in without the noise of the axe or hammer into the glorious building not made with hands. Everyone then must be polished here; and while there are many ways of doing this, the most effectual is suffering. And this is God's design in chastisement. This is what the Holy Spirit effects: as like a workman He stands over each stone, touching and retouching it, turning it on every side, marking its blemishes and roughness, and then applying His tools to effect the desired shape and polish. Some parts of the stone are so rugged and hard that nothing save heavy and repeated strokes and touches will smooth them down. They resist every milder treatment. And yet, in patient love, this heavenly Workman carries on the Father's purpose concerning us. Keeping beside Him, if one may thus speak after the manner of men, the perfect Model according to which the stone is to be fashioned – even Jesus, the Father's chosen One – He labours till every part is shaped according to His likeness, line after line. No pains are spared, no watchfulness relaxed, till we are made entirely like Him, being changed into the same image from glory to glory by the Spirit of the Lord.

Thus affliction moulds and purifies. Thus it effaces the resemblance of the first Adam and traces in us each lineament of the second that 'as we have borne the image of the earthly, we may also bear the image of the heavenly'. 'Oh,' said a saint of other days, 'what I owe to the file, to the hammer, to the furnace of my Lord Jesus!'

Come, then, let us question ourselves and endeavour to ascertain what affliction has been doing for us and what progress we are making in putting off the old man and in putting on the new. Am I leaving my worldliness of spirit and becoming heavenly minded? Am I getting rid of my pride, my passion, my stubbornness, and becoming humble, mild, and teachable? Are all my idols displaced and broken, and my creature comforts do I use as though I used them not? Am I caring less for the honours of time, for man's love, man's smile, man's applause? Am I crucified to the world and is the world crucified to me by the cross of Christ; or am I still ashamed of His reproach and am I half-reluctant to follow Him through bad report and through good, through honour and through shame? Do I count it my glory and my joy to walk where He has led the way, to suffer wherein He suffered, to drink of the cup of which He drank, and to be baptized with the baptism wherewith He was baptized? Or, while professing to seek the kingdom hereafter, do I refuse to undergo that tribulation through which I must enter; while willing to secure the crown of glory, do I shrink back from the crown of thorns? Am I every day becoming more and more unlike the children of earth, more and more fashioned after the likeness, and bearing the special lineaments, of my Elder Brother, of whom the whole family in Heaven and earth is named? Do I realize this earth as neither my portion nor my rest and, knowing that one chain may bind me as fast to the world as a thousand, am I careful to shake off every fetter that may bind me to the vanities of a world like this? Is chastisement really purifying me? Am I conscious of its blessed effects upon my soul? Can I look back upon such scenes of trial and say, 'There and then I learned most precious lessons; there and then I got rid of some of the body of this death; there and then I got up to a higher level from which I am striving to ascend to one higher still?' Have I learned much of the sympathy of Jesus and known the blessedness of having such a One as He to weep along with me in my day of sorrow? Have I wiped off my rebellious tears and been taught to shed only those of love and submissive fondness, tears of brotherhood and sympathy, tears of longing to be absent from the body and present with the Lord?

To make us 'partakers of his holiness' is God's great design as stated by the apostle. And there is something very remarkable about the expression. It corresponds to a similar one in the Second Epistle of Peter, 'partakers of the divine nature.' It implies something very exalted and very blessed; much more so than if it had merely been told us that God's aim was to 'make us holy'. Partakers of His own very holiness – His very nature! This is more than angels can glory in. It is something peculiar to 'the redeemed from among men' – the members of the Body of Christ. And it is in this way that Jesus speaks to us. It is not merely 'peace' that He promises to us, but His own peace – 'my peace'. It is not merely joy He bestows, but His own joy –'my joy.' So here it is not merely holiness He is conferring upon us, but His own holiness. His wish is to make us partakers of that. And oh, how much does that imply!

A goodly prize this – one for the obtaining of which we may well count all things but loss! It is well for us when we come to see it in all its value and excellency and to set our hearts upon it. Until we do so there will be strife between us and God, for this is the blessing which above all others He desires for us and which He is bent on conferring upon us. When, however, we come to be perfectly at one with Him as to this, then the struggle ceases. He gets His own way, and this is best for us. How blessed when His desire to deliver us from sin, and ours to be delivered from it, meet together; when His purpose to make us holy is cordially responded to by our fervent longings to be so! Then it is that the divine fullness flows into the soul without a check, and, notwithstanding the bitterness of the outward process by which this is effected, joy unspeakable and full of glory, possesses the consecrated soul.

'Wherefore, laying aside every weight, and the sin which doth so easily beset us, let us run with patience the race set before us, looking unto Jesus, the author and the finisher of our faith, who for the joy set before him endured the cross, despising the shame' (Heb. 12:1-2). And there is nothing like affliction for teaching us this. It acts like the wind upon the trees, making them take deeper root. It is the mowing of the grass that it may shoot up thicker and greener. It is the shaking of the torch that it may blaze the brighter.

# 10

# THE AROUSING

It may have been long since the Holy Spirit awoke us from our sleep of death. Into that same deep sleep we know that we shall never fall again. He who awoke us will keep us awake until Jesus come. In that sense we shall sleep no more.

But still much of our drowsiness remains. We are not wholly awake, and oftentimes much of our former sleep returns. Dwelling on the world's enchanted ground, our eyes close, our senses are bewildered, our conscience loses its sensitiveness, and our faculties their energy; we fall asleep even upon our watchtower, forgetful that the night is far spent, and the day is at hand.

While thus asleep, or half-asleep, all goes wrong. Our movements are sluggish and lifeless. Our faith waxes feeble; our love is chilled; our zeal cools down. The freshness of other years is gone. Our boldness has forsaken us. Our schemes are carelessly devised and drowsily executed. The work of God is hindered by us instead of being helped forward. We are a drag upon it. We mar it.

But God will not have it so. Neither for His work's sake nor for His saints' sake can He suffer this to continue. We must be aroused at whatsoever cost. We are not to be allowed to sleep as do others. We must watch and be sober, for we are children of the light and of the day, not of the night nor of darkness. God cannot permit us thus to waste life, as if its only use were to be sported with or trifled away. Duties lazily and lifelessly performed; half-hearted prayers; a deportment, blameless enough perhaps, but tame and unexpressive, and, therefore uninfluential; words well and wisely spoken perhaps but without weight – these are not things which God can tolerate in a saint. It is either the coldness of Sardis to which He says, 'If thou shalt not watch, I will come on thee as a thief, and thou shalt not know what hour I will come upon thee.' Or it is the lukewarmness of Laodicea to which He says, 'Because thou art lukewarm, and neither cold nor hot, I will spue thee out of my mouth.'

In arousing us God proceeds at first most gently. He touches us slightly, as the angel did Elijah under the juniper tree, that He may awaken us. He sends some slight visitation to shake us out of our security. He causes us to hear some distant noise: it may be the tumults of the nations, or it may be the tidings of famine, or war, or pestilence afar off. Perhaps this entirely fails; we slumber on as securely as ever. Our life is as listless and as useless as ever. Then He comes nearer, and makes His voice to be heard in our own neighbourhood or within the circle of our kindred. This also fails. Then He comes nearer still, for the time is hurrying on and the saint is still asleep. He speaks into our very ears. He smites upon some tender part till every fibre of our frame quivers and every pulse throbs quicker. Our very soul is stricken through as with a thousand arrows. Then we start up like one awakening out of a long sleep, and, looking round us, wonder how we could have slept so long.

But oh, how difficult it is to awaken us thoroughly! It needs stroke upon stroke in long succession to do this. For after every waking up there is the continual tendency to fall back into slumber. So that we need both to be made awake and to be kept awake. What sorrows does our drowsiness cost us – what bleeding, broken hearts! The luxury of 'ease in Zion' indulged in perhaps for years has been dearly bought.

'Think of living,' was the pregnant maxim of the thoughtful German. 'Thy life,' says another, quoting the above, 'wert thou the pitifullest of all the sons of earth, is no idle dream, but a solemn reality. It is thy own. It is all thou hast to confront eternity with. Work then, like a *star*, unhasting yet unresting.'

There are some Christians who work, but they do not work like men awake. They move forward in a certain track of duty, but it is with weary footstep. Their motions are constrained and cold.

They do many good things, devise many good schemes, say excellent things, but the vigorous pulse of warm life is wanting. Zeal, glowing zeal – elastic and untiring – is not theirs. They neither burn themselves, nor do they kindle others. There is nothing of the star about them save its coldness. They may expect some sharp stroke of chastisement, for they need it.

There are others who are only wakeful by fits and starts. They cannot be safely counted on, for their fervour depends upon the humour of the moment. A naturally impulsive temperament, of which, perhaps, they are not sufficiently aware, and which they have not sought either to crucify or to regulate, renders them uncertain in all their movements. This intermittent wakefulness effects but little. They do and they undo. They build up and they pull down. They kindle and quench the flame alternately. There is nothing of the 'star' about them. They stand in need of some sore and long continued pressure to equalize the variable, fitful movements of their spirit.

There are others who seem to be always wakeful, but then it is the wakefulness of bustle and restlessness. They cannot live but in the midst of stirring, and scheming, and moving to and fro. Their temperament is that nervous, tremulous impatient kind that makes rest or retirement to be felt as restraint and pain. These seldom effect much themselves, but they are often useful by their perpetual stir and friction for setting or keeping others in motion and preventing stagnation around them. But their incessant motion prevents their being filled with the needed grace. Their continual contact with the outward things of religion hinders their inward growth and mars their spirituality. These are certainly in one sense like the star, wakeful and unresting, but they move forward with such haste that instead of gathering light or giving it forth, they are losing every day the little that they possessed. A deep, sharp stroke will be needed for shaking off this false fervour and imparting the true calm wakefulness of spirit, to which, as saints, they are called. It is the deepening of spiritual feeling that is needed in their case, and it takes much chastening to accomplish this.

There are others who are always steadily at work and apparently with fervour too. Yet a little intercourse with them shows that they are not truly awake. They work so much more than they pray that they soon become like vessels without oil. They are farther on than the last class, yet still they need arousing. They are like the star, both 'unresting and unhasting', yet their light is dim. Its reflection upon a dark world is faint and pale. It is a deeper spiritual life and experience that they need; and for this, it may be, there is some sore visitation in store for them.

The true wakeful life is different from all these.

It is a thing of intensity and depth. It carries ever about with it the air of calm and restful dignity, of inward power and greatness. It is fervent, but not feverish; energetic, but not excited; speedy in its doings, but not hasty; prudent, but not timid or selfish; resolute and fearless but not rash; unobtrusive and sometimes, it may be, silent, yet making all around to feel its influence; full of joy and peace, yet without parade or noise; overflowing in tenderness and love, yet at the same time, faithful and true.

This is the wakeful life! But oh, before it is thoroughly attained, how much are we sometimes called upon to suffer through the rebelliousness of a carnal nature that will not let us surrender ourselves up wholly to God, and present ourselves as living sacrifices, which is our reasonable service!

In thus arousing us from our slumber, chastisement not merely makes us more energetic, more laborious, but it makes us far more prayerful. Perhaps it is here that the waking up is most sensibly felt. Nothing so quickens prayer as trial. It sends us at once to our knees and shuts the door of our closet behind us. In the day of prosperity we have many comforts, many refuges to resort to; in the day of sorrow we have only one, and that is God. Our grief is too deep to tell to any other; it is too heavy for any other to soothe. Now we awake to prayer. It was something to us before, but now it is all. Man's arm fails, and there is none but God to lean upon.

Our closets, in truth, are the only places of light in a world which has now become doubly dark to us. All without and around is gloom. Clouds overshadow the whole region. Only the closet is bright and calm. How eagerly, how thankfully we betake ourselves to it now! We could spend our whole time in this happy island of light which God has provided for us in the midst of a stormy ocean. When compelled at times to leave it, how gladly do we return to it! What peaceful hours of solitude we have there with God for our one companion! We can almost forget that the clouds of earth are still above us and its tempest still rioting around us.

Prayer becomes a far more real thing than ever. It is prized now as it was never prized before. We cannot do without it. Of necessity, as well as of choice, we must pray, sending up our cries from the depths. It becomes a real asking, a real pleading. It is no form now. What new life, new energy, new earnestness are poured into each petition! It is the heart that is now speaking, and the lips cannot find words wherewith to give utterance to its desires. The groanings that 'cannot be uttered' are all that now burst forth and ascend up into the ear of God. Formerly, there was often the lip without the heart; now it is far oftener the heart without the lip. Now we know how 'the

Spirit helpeth our infirmities'. We begin to feel what it is to 'pray in the Holy Ghost'.

There is a new nearness to God. Communion with Him is far more of a conscious reality now. It is close dealing with a living, personal Jehovah. New arguments suggest themselves; new desires spring up; new wants disclose themselves. Our own emptiness and God's manifold fullness are brought before us so vividly that the longings of our inmost souls are kindled, and our heart crieth out for God, for the living God. It was David's sorrows that quickened prayer in him. It was in the belly of the whale that Jonah was taught to cry aloud. And it was among the thorns of the wilderness and the fetters of Babylon that Manasseh learned to pray.

Church of Christ – chosen heritage of the Lord – awake! Children of the light and of the day, arise! The long winter night is nearly over. The day-star is preparing to ascend. 'The end of all things is at hand: be ye therefore sober, and watch unto prayer' (1 Pet. 4:7). 'Why sleep ye? rise and pray, lest ye enter into temptation!' (Luke 22:46).

# 11

# THE SOLEMNIZING

Laughter and gaiety belong to a fallen world. They are too superficial to have place among the holy; and too hollow to be known among the truly happy. With the peace of God in our hearts we feel that we do not need them. They may do for childhood; they may do for the world; but not for us. They do not suit our feelings; they are not deep or solid enough to be in harmony with our new nature. They are not the utterances of a truly happy soul.

Yet we live in a gay world that rings everywhere with hollow laughter. Around us are the sights and sounds of mirth by which vain men are seeking to cheat away their ever-fretting uneasiness, to soothe their ruffled consciences, or to drown their bitter sorrows. Oftentimes the saints seem to catch the tone of levity, making mirth with the most mirthful, jesting with the most foolish, singing, perhaps, the world's songs of vanity, speaking its idle words, walking in its vain paths as if its friendships and pleasures were not forbidden things.

Apart, however, from the contagion of the world's influence our tone is apt to fall low and our deportment to lose that solidity and seriousness which become the saints. Almost unconsciously and without knowing how, we get light and airy; we give way to the current of vain thoughts; we forget to set a guard upon our lips; we indulge in foolish talking and jesting in our meetings with each other. Our words are not 'with grace seasoned with salt'. We forget the admonition, 'Let no corrupt communication proceed out of your mouths, but that which is good to the use of edifying, that I may minister grace to the hearers.'

This propensity grows upon us. Seriousness becomes a thing reserved entirely for the closet or the sanctuary. We forget our character as saints, called out of darkness and 'delivered from a present evil world'. We lose sight of our heavenly parentage and divine adoption. Our whole habits of thought, feeling, speaking, and doing too much resemble the flippancies of a heedless, light-hearted world, whose maxim is, 'Let us eat, drink, and be merry.'

Thus our spirituality decays. Heavenly mindedness is gone. We become of the earth, earthly. Our souls cleave to the dust, and we are content to grovel there. We become lean and barren, neither growing ourselves nor helping the growth of others. Our blossoms send forth no fragrance, our branches bear no fruit.

We grieve the Holy Spirit of God whereby

we are sealed unto the day of redemption. He cannot dwell with levity and mirth any more than amid profanity and crime. He retires from the temple into which He had come and in which He would fain make His abode forever, driven out from it by the laughter and jesting with which we were making its consecrated walls to resound. How can He dwell in a temple which from being a house of God and a house of prayer, we have turned into a place of merchandise, a hall of revelry, a haunt of mirth and song?

I do not mean, as I have said before, that the saint is ever to be gloomy. No. Gloom and melancholy are not our portion. 'The lines have fallen unto us in pleasant places.' They are not the inmates of a soul that has tasted the joy of pardon and is walking in light, as a happy child with a loving father. But true joy is a serious thing. Its fountains are deep. It is the waking up of the heart's deep springs. Mirth and levity are not joy. They are too shallow to deserve the name. Like the sun-flash on a stagnant pool, they are a mere surface gleam of light. There is nothing in them of the calm radiance illuminating the ocean depths many a fathom down, as if the waters themselves were a mass of solid sunshine, and remaining amid the heaving of the billows, unbroken and unobscured. In coming to Him, who is the fountain of all gladness, the saint of God bids farewell to gloom. Tribulation he may have

– nay, must have – but not gloom. That has left him forever since the day he knew the Saviour, and opened his ears to the joyful sound. Peace is now his heritage.

But still it is not levity that is his portion. It is joy. And this joy is not only far superior to this vain mirth but it is utterly inconsistent with it. This levity is as much an enemy to real joy as it is to holiness and spirituality. Hence, it must be rooted up. God cannot suffer it in His children. His desire is that they should set their affections on things above. This element of earthliness must be purged out. They must be made solemn and thoughtful. To this end He visits them with chastisement. In a moment, perhaps, He smites them to the dust; or, by some slower but withering, crushing calamity, He slays and casts out that foolishness which had wrought itself into the very texture of their being.

His purpose is to make them thoughtful and solemn. He lays on them accordingly something that will make them think. The blow prostrates them, and in a moment all levity is put to flight. They cannot laugh and jest now when their home is desolate and their heart is bleeding. They are withdrawn from intercourse with an airy, shadowy world and sent into the very inmost recesses of their spiritual being, or forward to the infinite eternity, whose vastness they had been but little alive to.

Trials awaken us to a sense of our self-pleasing ways and our indifference to the condition of the world we live in, not only as being a world of sin, but thoroughly, and all over, a world of misery. They bring us into contact with solid certainties and that produces thoughtfulness. They make us 'acquainted with grief' and that drives off all levity. Sorrow and levity keep no companionship.

It is through tears that truth is best seen. When looked at through this medium, objects assume their right proportions and take their proper level. Shadows then evaporate. Realities compass us about and these make us solemn. Shadows only make us light and vain. They never stir the depths of our being, but merely flit around its surface.

Thus God solemnizes His saints, and brings them in this respect into closer sympathy with the mind of Christ. All was solemnity with Him. There was no levity ever found in Him. Everything about Him was serene, yet everything was solemn. And the nearer we are brought to resemble Him, the more will this calm, happy solemnity possess us. We shall live not only wakeful but solemn lives. Our whole deportment will speak the depth of the serenity that dwells within. Our looks and tones will all be solemn, and will of themselves testify for God and condemn the world. We shall be men awake and alive, men zealous and in earnest; men who have no relish for levity, because it is incompatible with the deep peace which is their better portion, and who feel that they have no time for it, because eternity is so near.

Yes, a near eternity rebukes and banishes frivolity. Even apart from positive trial this is its tendency. It is the eternal lifetime that makes the lifetime of earth such a solemn thing. Sever the living here from the living hereafter, and man's longest time on earth is little more in importance than the flutter of a leaf, his death no more than the falling of a blossom. But fasten on the infinite and the eternal to our present existence, and everything in life becomes mighty, momentous, solemn. The briefest moment that comes and goes is the meeting place of two eternities. Traversing this narrow pass, with rocks on either side of infinite ascent and lost in impenetrable midnight, how can we fail to be solemnized unless our eyes be closed or our reason gone!

The pang that shoots through our frame and makes each fibre quiver would be quite endurable were it but for a moment, were it to die and be buried with us in the same tomb, were there no capacity of eternal anguish in our nature, or no eternity in which that capacity must develop itself. The sting of a moment is a trifle, but the eternal stinging of the undying worm is terrific beyond all utterance. In like manner the thrill of fresh joy which makes the whole man throb with delight would scarce be worth the having or the losing were it only like the lightning, flashing out in its brightness and then quenched for ever. But a nature gifted with faculties for infinite enjoyment, and with a whole eternity in which these joyous buds shall expand themselves, turns all our life into a deep and awful reality. A flower that folds up its leaves and withers down at sunset may be carelessly trodden underfoot; but a star that shall roll around forever in its orbit, either effulgent in beauty or dark in the gloom of its own chaos, is an object of wonder and awe.

Such is the life of man! Not the life of one man or some men, but of every man. By itself it may seem a plaything, a mere insect's life; but in connection with the everlasting future, it becomes awfully real and solemn in its aspect. We may be noble and famed upon the earth, or we may be poor, unlettered, hard-toiling men, still our life is a vast reality. It is no mere shadow, or rainbow, or vision of the night, but an inconceivable reality in all its parts, great or small.

Such especially is the life of the saint! He not only knows that there is an eternity, but he has seen and felt it. Each hour he is looking out upon it like a traveller looking over a dark and infinite precipice which flanks the road on which he is passing along. He not only knows that there is such a thing as forgiveness and eternal life, but he has found them, he has tasted them; his eyes have been opened, and he has now come into the very midst of realities. They compass him about on every side. And especially as he 'looks for that blessed hope, even the glorious appearing' of the Lord, he feels what a solemn life he is called upon to lead, and levity and mirth as ill become him as they would have done the high priest, when standing within the veil under the immediate vision of the glory.

Even without the positive infliction of chastisement there is enough to solemnize a saint in what he sees and knows of things as they are. A dying world, a groaning creation, a curse-laden earth, a divided, bleeding church, an absent bridegroom – these are at all times enough to subdue and soften a believer's frame. And thus he walks through earth like Paul after he had been in the third heaven – an inhabitant of another star – one who has his conversation in heaven – who is too happy ever to be gloomy, but too happy also ever to be light or vain.

# 12

# THE WARNING

Affliction is full of warnings. It has many voices and these of the most various kinds. It speaks counsel, it speaks rebuke, it speaks affection. But it speaks warning too. Let us hear some of its words of warning.

*1. It says, 'Love not the world,* neither the things that are in the world. If any man love the world, the love of the Father is not in him' (1 John 2:15). There is no enforcement of this warning so solemn as that which affliction gives. It exposes the world's hollowness and says, 'love not.' It shows us what a withering gourd its beauty is and says, 'love not.' It points out to us its hastening doom and says, 'love not.' It declares the utter impossibility of loving both the world and the Father. 'If any man love the world, the love of the Father is not in him.' 'Know ye not that the friendship of the world is enmity with God?' There can be no companionship between God and the world. They cannot dwell together under the same roof or in the same heart.

*2. It says, 'Take heed and beware of covetousness'* (Luke 12:15). Riches cannot help, neither earthly comfort avail us in the hour of grief. They cannot dry up tears, nor reunite broken bonds, they cannot heal the living, nor bring back the dead. They profit not in the day of darkness. Their vanity and emptiness cannot then be hidden. 'Thou fool, this night thy soul shall be required of thee. Then whose shall those things be which thou hast provided?' It is then we find that we need a 'treasure in the heaven that faileth not'. 'I counsel thee to buy of *me* gold tried in the fire, that thou mayest be rich.'

3. *It says, 'Abstain from all appearance of evil'* (1 Thess. 5:22). 'Hate even the garments spotted by the flesh.' It is not the flesh merely that we are to hate, but even its garments. Nor is it the garments dyed and defiled with the flesh, but even 'spotted' with it. It is not merely abstain from evil, but from all appearance of evil. Suffering teaches us to shrink from sin – even from the remotest and most indirect connection with it. It says, 'Oh, do not that abominable thing which I hate!'

4. *It says, 'Grudge not one against another'* (James 5:9). Let there be no half-hearted affection in the family of God. Let there be no envy, no jealousy, no misunderstandings among the brethren. Why should we be less than friends who are both fellow-sufferers and fellow-soldiers here? Why should we, who are sharers in a common danger and a common exile, bear for each other aught but the sympathies of an intense

affection? Why should we not love one another with a pure heart fervently? Yet oftentimes it needs affliction to teach us this, to remove our jealousies, and to draw us together as brethren in sympathy and love.

5. *It says, 'Keep yourselves from idols'* (1 John 5:21). If there be one remaining idol, break it in pieces and spare it not. Nothing is so fruitful a cause of suffering as idolatry. Nothing so forcibly displays the vanity of our idols as suffering. It is with this whip of cords that Christ scourges out of us the buyers and sellers – suffering no earthly traffic to proceed in His Father's house.

I give these warnings merely as specimens, a few out of many which might be adduced. There is no room for citing more, though more might easily be found. The two great points against which the warnings of chastisement are directed seem to be selfishness and worldliness. To scourge these thoroughly out of us is God's design.

1. *Selfishness.* 'All seek their own, not the things that are Jesus Christ's.' This was Paul's complaint, not of the ungodly, but of the churches of Christ. It was the selfishness he saw in the saints that gave occasion to these sorrowful words.

This selfishness is of various kinds, and shows itself in various ways. It is selfishness in reference to the things of Christ; or in reference to the

125

Church of Christ; or in reference to the work given us to do; or in reference to the sacrifices we are called upon to undergo, and the toils we are called upon to endure. It would be easy to show how God's chastisements are pointed at all these forms of selfishness, aiming deadly blows at each one of them from the outermost to the innermost circle. But this is too large a field. We shall merely take up the first, and even it we can only touch upon. It is the most important of them all, and stands so connected with the rest that whatever uproots it destroys the others also.

Selfishness, in reference to the things of Christ, obviously springs from coldness towards Christ Himself. A preference of self to Christ is its root and source. Anything, therefore, that tends to obscure or keep out of view the person of Christ must lead to selfishness. It may be the love of the world; it may be the love of the creature; it may be the love of man's applause. These are the dark bodies that eclipse the glory of a living Saviour and nourish self. But these are not all. Satan has deeper devices still. He brings in religion between us and the Saviour! Religious acts, ordinances, duties, are all turned by him into so many instruments for exalting self and lowering the Saviour. But even this is not all. He has a subtler device still for these last days. He is trying to make the work of Christ a substitute for His person, to fix attention so much upon the one as to exclude the other. The result of this is a thoroughly selfish and sectarian religion. I know this is delicate ground, but the evil is an augmenting one and ought to be made known.

There are not a few who are so occupied with truth that they forget 'the true one', so occupied with faith that they lose sight of its personal object, so given to dwelling upon the work of Christ that they overlook His person. They seem to regard the latter subject as a matter, if not beyond them, at least one about which it will be time enough to concern themselves when they see Him face to face. What He is seems a question of small importance, provided they know that He has accomplished a work by which they may secure eternal life. 'We are forgiven,' they say, 'we have peace – all is well.' They take but little interest in the person of Him who has purchased these blessings. The redemption is all, and the Redeemer is nothing, or, at least, very little! The sufficiency of His work is all, the glory and excellence of His person, nothing! What is this but selfishness? We get all the benefit we can out of the work of Christ, and then leave Him alone! And this selfishness introduces itself everywhere into the actions and thinking of this class. We can trace it in the mould of their doctrines. Their views of the atonement are selfish, being framed not upon the principle of how God is to get His purpose fulfilled and His glory displayed, but simply of how a sinner is to be saved. Their views of Jehovah's sovereignty and electing grace are selfish, being just so many devices for taking the sinner out of God's hands and placing him in his own. Their views of the Spirit's work are selfish, being just an attempt to make His aid appear less absolutely indispensable and man's own skill and strength of very considerable avail in the matter of salvation. But even where those selfish views of doctrine have not been adopted, there is a latent tendency toward selfishness among many, which can only be ascribed to their neglect of the person of Christ.

But what has chastisement to do with this? Much every way. Chiefly in this that it throws us more entirely for consolation and strength upon the person of the Saviour. Never do we feel more brought into contact with a living personal Saviour than in our days of sorrow. It is Jesus – Jesus alone – Jesus Himself – whom we feel to be absolutely necessary. The truth is precious; His work is precious; but it is with Him that we have chiefly to do; it is to Him that we pour out our sorrows.

Thus by creating a necessity for our leaning on the person of Jesus (blessed necessity!) affliction strikes at that which was the root of selfishness. By bringing before us another and far more glorious self, it absorbs our own miserable self, till in the person of Jesus we lose sight of our own selves altogether. There is nothing that so makes us acquainted with Christ Himself as sorrow; and hence, there is nothing so efficacious in eradicating self. It is God's cure for selfishness. It is His way of making us seek, not our own, but the things that are Jesus Christ's. It is His way of carrying us beyond truth even to 'him that is true'. Truth is precious, but in itself it is cold. But the glory of the gospel is this that it carries us up beyond truth to its living fountain-head. Nay, it brings us into the very bosom of Him who came out of the Father's bosom and has now returned to it carrying with Him all those whom the Father hath given Him, there, with Him to abide in happy fellowship, world without end.

This, however, is a large subject, and these are but a few hints. We cannot, however, pursue them further here. We pass on to notice the other evil against which the rebukes of God are directed.

*2. Worldliness.* We have seen that God's cure for selfishness is the setting before us of another self to absorb our own in the person of Jesus. We have now to see that His cure for worldliness is the bringing before us of another world, more glorious than that which He calls on us to forsake. There is no thorough cure for it but this. It is want of faith that makes us worldlings; and when the believing eye gets fixed on the world to come, then we learn to set our affections on things above. So long, however, as all here is bright, we are content with them; we allow ourselves to sink down and settle quietly among the things of earth. But when God unroofs our dwelling, or tears up its foundation by an earthquake, then we are forced to look upward and seek a better and more enduring portion. Many such shocks, however, are often needed before our souls are broken off from their cleaving to the dust.

The opposite of worldliness is heavenly mindedness or spiritual mindedness. This, the new relish which the Holy Spirit imparts at conversion, in some measure produces. But it is feeble. It easily gives way. It is not *keen* enough to withstand much temptation. God's wish is to impart a keener relish for the things of God and to destroy the relish for the things of time. This He effects by *blighting* all objects in which there was earthly sweetness, so that by being deprived of objects to 'mind' on earth, it may of necessity be led to 'mind' the things above. He dries up all the 'nether springs' of earthly joy, that we may betake ourselves to the 'upper springs' which can never fail.

There is much worldliness among the saints. There is worldliness in their motives and actions, worldliness in their domestic life and in their intercourse with society, there is worldliness in the arrangements of their households and in the education of their families; there is worldliness in their expenditure, so much being laid out for self, so little for God; there is worldliness in their religious schemes, and movements and societies; there is worldliness in their reading, and in their conversation; there is, in short, too much of the spirit of *earnest worldliness* about their whole deportment, and very little of calm, happy superiority to the things of earth. They are fretted, disturbed, bustled just like the world. They grudge labour, or fatigue, or expense, or annoyance in the cause of Christ, or in serving their fellowmen. They have much of earth, little of Heaven about them. They are not large-hearted, open-handed – willing to spend and be spent, unmoved and unruffled, as those whose eye is ever set on the incorruptible inheritance on which they so soon shall enter. They are low and unaspiring in the things of God.

Perhaps there are few things against which we require to be more warned than against this spirit of worldliness. The Church is very prone to forget her pilgrim character in this present evil world and to live as a citizen of earth. Her dignity as the eternally chosen of the Father is lost sight of; her hope as the inheritor of the glory and the kingdom of the Son is obscured. And oh, how much of sorrow she is preparing for herself by thus losing sight of her calling! What desolation may be even now hovering over the tabernacle of many a saint, because they will not come out and be separate, because they refuse to be 'strangers on the earth as all their fathers were'. Sad it is, indeed, that we should need affliction to teach us this!

Why should we, whose home and treasure are above, ever again seek our home or our treasure here? Why should we stoop from our heavenly elevation to mingle again with the company which we have forsaken? Have we repented of our choice? Are we ashamed of our pilgrim staff and our pilgrim weeds? Surely not. Oh, if to be a stranger on earth is to be divided from sin and sinful appetites, from the seducing vanities and worthless mockeries of the world, from the fascinating beauty and perilous splendour of this decaying scene – if to be a stranger on earth is to be a friend of God, a member of the heavenly household, an expectant of the kingdom, an heir apparent of the crown of glory – who would not be a stranger here?

What higher honour would we seek than to share the homelessness of Jesus, the homelessness of the Church from the beginning? Why should we seek to enter into nearer fellowship and dearer relationship with such a world as this? If we knew of no fairer heritage, we might not be wondered at for lusting after our forsaken pleasures. But we have the pleasures that are at God's right hand forever, and what are earth's allurements to us? What to us are the sights and sounds of earth, who 'shall see the king in his beauty,' and hear His voice, into whose lips grace is poured? What to us is the green fertility of earth, who shall enter into the possession of the new earth, when 'the winter is past, the rain over and gone'? What to us is the gay glory of a city's wealth and pomp, who shall be made citizens of the New Jerusalem, where dwells the glory of God and of the Lamb, whose foundations are of precious stones, whose walls are of jasper, whose gates are of pearl, whose streets and pavements are of transparent gold?

Let us, then, 'pass the time of our sojourning here in fear.' Let our loins be girt about and our lamps burning, and let us be as men ready to go forth to meet our returning Lord. If we watch not, if we reject the warning, our chastisement will be sharp and sore.

The present seems a time of peculiar warning to the saints. Many are lying under the rebukes of the Lord. Judgment has begun at the house of God. God is dealing very closely and very solemnly with His own. On many a saint at this moment is His rod lying heavily, for He would fain warn and arouse them ere the evil day arrive. He is dealing with them as He dealt with Lot on the night before the desolation of Sodom. Let the saints, then, be warned. Let them be zealous and repent and do their first works. Come out, be separate, touch not the unclean thing! Put off the works of darkness; put on the armour of light. He is calling on them to get up on a higher level in the spiritual life, to have done with wavering, indecision, and compromise. He is calling on them to consider the apostle and High Priest of their profession and walk in His steps. He is calling on them to look at that cloud of witnesses, and lay aside every weight, especially that sin (of unbelief) which doth so easily beset them, and to run with patience the race set before them – 'looking unto Jesus.'

Church of the living God! Be warned. Please not thyself, even as Jesus pleased not Himself. Live for Him, not for thyself, for Him, not for the world. Walk worthy of thy name and calling, worthy of Him who bought thee as His bride, worthy of thine everlasting inheritance.

Up, too, and warn the world! The chastisements that are falling so thickly on thee are forerunners of the fiery shower that is preparing for the earth. Up, then, and warn them – urge and entreat them to flee from gathering wrath. They have no time to lose, neither hast thou. The last storm is on the wing. Its dark skirts are already visible in the heavens. Judgment has begun at the house of God, and if so, what shall the end be of them that obey not the gospel of God!

# 13

## THE RECOLLECTIONS

'He hath made his wonderful works to be remembered' (Ps. 111:4). Yes, they are for 'everlasting remembrance'. They are not meant to be forgotten, and therefore, they are so *made* as to render forgetfulness almost impossible. Still we lose sight of them. They pass away 'like a tale that is told'.

Among the most wonderful of God's works are His chastisements. *They* are to be specially remembered by us. In themselves they are worthy of this. In their connection with us more so. None are so ineffaceable, for none are written so deep upon the heart. They are entwined with all that we feared or hoped in other days. They are 'graven with an iron pen, and with lead in the rock for ever'. No pen is like that of sorrow for writing indelibly upon the soul.

Simple as sorrow God's dealings with us are not likely to be soon forgotten. We take pleasure in recalling our tears and griefs. But this is often mere selfish melancholy, brooding in solitude over a strange history. Sometimes, too, it is pride. We take proud pleasure in thinking that none has ever suffered as we have done. Sometimes it is worldly *sentiment*, sitting down to muse over faded blossoms, or to recall the images of suns long set, or it may be to contrast the decay of earth with the abiding beauty of yon unwrinkled azure.

But this is not what God desires. It is not merely the remembrance of sorrow that He seeks, but of sorrow as chastisement – or sorrow as linked all along with His gracious dealings toward us. The natural heart separates these two things. It remembers the one but forgets the other and so frustrates God's design. *Himself* He ever presents to us; *Himself* He strives to keep before us, not simply as connected with all our present and all our future history, but as inseparably entwined with all the *past*.

It was thus that He expressed His mind to Israel regarding this very thing. 'Thou shalt remember all the way which the LORD thy God led thee these forty years in the wilderness, to humble thee, and to prove thee, to know what was in thine heart, whether thou wouldest keep his commandments, or no. And he humbled thee, and suffered thee to hunger, and fed thee with manna, which thou knewest not, neither did thy fathers know; that he might make thee know that man doth not live by bread only, but by every word that proceedeth out of the mouth of the LORD doth man live. Thy raiment waxed not old upon thee, neither did thy foot swell these forty years. Thou shalt also consider in thine heart, that, as a man chasteneth his son, so the LORD thy God chasteneth thee' (Deut. 8:2-5).

These recollections of the wilderness He wished to write upon Israel's heart forever. He evidently lays much stress on this. He would not have them lose the benefit of their desert wanderings, and His desert dealings. They were too precious to be forgotten. Forty years close and solitary intercourse with God in such various ways ought to have taught them much, both of Him and of themselves, which deserved everlasting memory. Each name had some wondrous scene attached to it; each rock had its story to tell. Their enemies and dangers, their hunger and their thirst, the manna and the water, the murmurings and the thanksgiving, their journeys and their encampments, their raiment that waxed not old, their shoes that were as iron and brass, their feet that swelled not, and above all, the cloud that rested over them, and the tent of Jehovah that was pitched in the midst of them – these were memorable scenes. And they were all connected with the wilderness. Never before had there been such an assemblage of wondrous dealings, and never since has anything like this been seen on earth. It could occur but once. And that once was to furnish matter for remembrance to Israel, descending as a precious heritage to their children and to their children's children forever.

It is thus with the saint in reference to his desert days and desert trials. They must not be forgotten as if they had served their purpose. They must be ever rising before us – not merely preserved in memory like the manna in the ark, but brought forth to feed upon every day. In this way sorrow may be most profitable to us long after its bitterness has passed away. It may furnish us with a treasury of blessings for a lifetime. It may be a mine of gold to us all our days. We are too little aware of this. We look on trial too much as we do upon a passing shower, which falls and then is gone. Whereas, it is truly the smiting of the rock and the issuing forth of a new stream, whose waters are to keep us company through all our days of wandering. The benefits of chastisement should never be exhausted. They should be coming forth in freshness with every hour. Even when sitting calmly in the sunshine we may be drawing profit from the stormy past. This is consolation to the chastened soul; for how often in this way will a short sorrow be turned into lasting gladness. And it does seem as if what is thus obtained by us were a richer kind of blessing, a holier, deeper joy. Oh, let us remember past trials and carefully treasure them up as the choicest of our earthly possessions! The saint who has many of these to look back upon has some reason to glory in his inheritance.[1]

---

1. 'Truly no cross should be old to us. We should not forget them, because years are come betwixt us and them, and cast them by hand as we do old clothes. We may make a cross old in time new in use, and as fruitful as in the beginning of it' (Samuel Rutherford).

It is this that especially exercises that softening, mellowing influence which has been often observed in affliction. During the actual pressure of the sorrow there was less of this. Perhaps we were so stunned and stupefied as almost to be deprived of feeling. Or if we did feel, still there was so much of sharpness and bitterness about it that we were bruised rather than softened. There was such a struggle and such confusion of spirit that we sometimes wondered if we were profiting at all, and thought that the sorrow was too great to be productive of benefit.

But in the retrospect all is different. 'No chastening *for the present* seemeth to be joyous but grievous; nevertheless, *afterwards* it yieldeth the peaceable fruits of righteousness unto them which are exercised thereby.' The wound has ceased to bleed, and, though it will remain a scar forever, it is no longer open. It is then that the mellowing process goes on, and each remembrance of the past helps it forward. This is less perceptible than the others; we are not so directly conscious of it; but its silent influence upon our character, our temper, our will, our judgment, is wonderful. The deathbed, the farewell, the funeral scene, the open tomb, the earth striking rudely on the coffin, the grave filled up, the turf rolled on by stranger hands – these are like swords going through the very vitals. But they sadden more than they soften. It is the *remembrance* of these scenes, the frequent visit to the closed tomb, the calm after inquiry into, and meditation upon, God's meaning in all this – it is these that so gently exercise a whole lifetime's influence upon the soul. They surround us with a softening atmosphere, and the light they shed down on us is the light of sunset, mellowed and shaded in its passage through the clouds of evening.

In another way also these recollections are precious. They teach us that God is *true*. The trials themselves taught us this; but their remembrance teaches us this more. And it is a lesson which even the saints need much to learn. Even they need to be taught how surely He is the *Amen,* 'the faithful and the true,' and in all that He has spoken to His Church He has spoken *truly*. What refreshing confirmations of this do we gather as we call to mind the past and see how the Lord hath led us! We can add our Amen every day to what Joshua declared to Israel on his deathbed. 'Behold, this day I am going the way of all the earth: and ye know in all your hearts and in all your souls, that not one thing hath failed of all the good things which the LORD your God spake concerning you; all are come to pass unto you, and not one thing hath failed thereof' (Josh. 23:14).

Yes, 'all things work together for good' – the past as well as the present. And thus the stream of which we drink is a swelling one. Innumerable

140

tributaries are flowing into it. This year it is 'to the ankles'. Next year it will be 'to the knees'. After that it will rise 'to the loins'. And as it reaches the ocean, bearing us calmly on its bosom, it will be a great river 'that cannot be passed over'.

Yet, oh, how little have the saints learned to prize these memorials of chastisement, these recollections of the wilderness, which are so rich in instruction, so fraught with blessing and with joy!

# 14

# THE CONSOLATION

'To bring many sons unto glory' was the end for which the Son of God took flesh and died. This was no common, no inferior object. So vast and worthy did Jehovah deem it that it pleased Him for the attaining of it to 'make the captain of their salvation perfect through sufferings' (Heb. 2:10). It was an object worthy of the God 'for whom are all things, and by whom are all things'. It was an object glorious enough to render it 'becoming' in Him to make Jesus pass through suffering and death, and to justify the Father in not sparing His only begotten Son.

They for whom God has done all this must be very precious in His sight. He must be much in earnest indeed to bless them and to take them to be with Him forever. As He so delighted in Enoch that He could no longer bear the separation and the distance, but took him to be with Him without tasting death, and long ere he had run the common race of man, so with His saints. He is making haste to bring them to glory, for the day of absence has been long.

The glory which He has in reserve for them must be surpassing glory, for it was to bring them to it that He was willing to bruise His Son and to put Him to grief. Eye hath not seen it; ear hath not heard it; it is far beyond what we can comprehend, yet it is all reality. God is not ashamed to be called our God because He hath prepared for us a city. Were that city not worthy of Himself He would be ashamed to have called Himself by the name of 'our God'. For that implies large blessings on His part, and it leads to large expectations on ours, expectations which He cannot disappoint.

He did not count this glory to be bought for us at too dear a rate, even though the price was the sufferings of His begotten Son. If, then, God thus estimated the glory to which we were to be brought, shall not we do the same? If *He* thought it worth all the sufferings of His Son, shall *we* not think it worth our poor sufferings here? Shall we not say, 'I reckon that the sufferings of this present time are not worthy to be compared with the glory which shall be revealed in us' (Rom. 8:18).

This is consolation. It is that which most naturally occurs to us, and it is both scriptural and effectual. This is what is usually presented to the afflicted saint, and it is what he feels to be very precious and suitable. But though the most common and the most natural consolation, it is by no means the only one. Let us suggest a few others.

*1. Jesus weeps with us.* 'In *all* our affliction he is afflicted.' He knows our sorrows, for He has passed through them all, and therefore He feels for us. He is touched with the feeling of our griefs as well as of our infirmities. Man – very man – man all over, even in His glory He enters most fully into the fellowship of our burdens and sorrows, whatever these may be, for there is not one which He did not taste when He 'dwelt among us' here. His is sympathy, deep, real, and true. It is no fiction, no fancy. We do not see His tears falling upon us; neither do we clasp His hand nor feel the beating of His heart against ours. But still His communion with us in suffering is a reality. We may not understand how it can be. But *He* understands it; and He can make us *feel* it, whether we can comprehend it or not.

*2. We are made partakers of Christ's sufferings.* What honour is this! We are baptized with His baptism; we drink of His cup, we are made like Him in sorrow as we shall hereafter be made like Him in joy! How soothing and sustaining! If reproach, and shame, and poverty are ours, let us remember that they were His also. If we have to go down to Gethsemane, or up to the cross, let us think that He was there before us. It is when keeping our eye on this that we are brought somewhat to realize the feeling of the apostle when he 'rejoiced in his suffering' for the Church, as filling 'up that which is behind [literally the leavings of Christ's sufferings] of the afflictions of Christ in my flesh for his body's sake, which is the church' (Col. 1:24). To be treated better than Christ was is neither what a thoughtful soul could expect, nor what a loving heart could desire.

3. *Suffering is the family lot.* This we have already dwelt upon, and we recur to it simply to present it more prominently as a *consolation*. The path of sorrow is no unfrequented way. All the saints have trodden it. We can trace their footprints there. It is comforting, nay, it is cheering to keep this in mind. Were we cast fettered into some low dungeon, would it not be consolation to know that many a martyr had been there before us, would it not be cheering to read their names written with their own hands all round the ancient walls? Such is the solace we may extract from *all* suffering, for the furnace into which we are cast has been consecrated by many a saint already.

4. *All things work together for our good.* Nothing is unsuitable, unseasonable, or unprofitable. Out of all evil comes good to the saints; out of all darkness comes light; out of all sorrow comes joy. Each pang, sharp or slight, is doing its work – the very work which God designs, the very work which we could not do without. The bed of sorrow is not only like Solomon's chariot, all 'paved with love,' but, like

it, it moves on with mighty swiftness, bearing us most blessedly onward to the inheritance of the undefiled. The *forces* of earth, unless they all bear in one line, or nearly so, tend to counteract each other and arrest the common impulse. Come from what quarter they may, or from opposite quarters all at once, they still bear us successfully forward. 'All things work together for good.' 'All things are ours.'

5. *There is special grace for every trial.* As trials bring to light the weakness that is in us, so they draw out to meet the strength of God – new resources of strength and grace which we never knew before. In affliction we may be quite sure of learning something more of God than we were acquainted with before, for it is just in order to furnish an opportunity for bringing out this and showing it to us that He sends the trial. How little should we know of Him were it not for sorrow! What fullness of blessing comes out to us, what riches of love are spread out before us in the dark and cloudy day!

6. *Affliction is our fullest opportunity for glorifying God.* It is on earth that He expects to get glory from us, glory such as angels cannot give, glory such as we shall not be able to give hereafter. It is *here* that we are to preach to angels; it is *here* we are to show to them what a glorious God is ours. Our whole life below is given us for this. But it is especially in sorrow and under

infirmity that God looks for glory from us. What a God-honouring thing to see a struggling, sorrowing child of earth cleave fast to God, calmly trusting in Him, happy and at rest in the midst of storm and of suffering! What a spectacle for the hosts of Heaven! Now, then, is the time for the saints to give glory to the Lord their God. Let them prize affliction as the very time and opportunity for doing so most of all. Let them use such a season well. And oh, what consolation to think that affliction is really such a season! Ah, surely it is one which an angel might covet, which an archangel would gladly stoop to were that possible! *They* can glorify God much in Heaven amid its glory and blessedness, but oh, not half so much as *we* can on earth amid suffering and shame!

7. *We are getting rid of sin.* Each pain is a nail driven through some sin, another blow inflicted on the flesh, destroying the very power of sinning. As we entered on our first life, sin fastened its chain upon us, and link after link twined itself about us. When we commenced our second and better life, these began one by one to untwine themselves. Affliction untwined them faster; and though it is not till we are laid on the deathbed, or till Jesus come, that the last link of earth is thoroughly untwined or broken, still it is consolation to think that each successive trial is helping on the blessed consummation. A

lifetime's sufferings would not be too long or too heavy, if by means of them we got rid of sin and sinful ways and tempers, and became more holy, more heavenly, more conformable to the image of the Lord. When first we believed in Jesus we were 'delivered from a present evil world'. Yet this deliverance is not complete. The world and we have not yet fully parted company with each other. And, therefore, God drives affliction like a wedge between us and our world; or He sends it like a ploughshare right across our most cherished hopes and brightest prospects till He thoroughly wearies us of all below. 'He hath made me weary,' said Job. Nor do we wonder at the complaint. Wearisome nights were his. The 'ploughers ploughed upon his back,' and drew many a long furrow there. He might well be weary. So with us. God makes us weary, too, weary all over – thoroughly weary. We get weary of a present evil world, weary of self, weary of sin, weary of suffering, weary of this mortal body, weary of these vile hearts, weary of earth – weary of all but Jesus! Of Him no trial can weary us. Suffering only endears Him the more. Blessed suffering – that makes Him appear more precious and the world viler; that brings Him nearer to our hearts and thrusts the world away!

8. *We are preparing for usefulness while here.* We have but a few years below, and it concerns us much that these should be *useful* years. We

have but *one* life, and it must be laid out for God. But we need *preparation* for usefulness. We need a thorough breaking down, a thorough emptying, a thorough bruising. God cannot trust us with success till we are thus laid low. We are not fit to receive it; nor would He get the glory. Therefore He sends sore and heavy trials in order to make us vessels fit for the Master's use. And oftentimes we see that the heaviest trials are forerunners of our greatest usefulness. When we are entirely prostrated and crushed, then it is *safe* to grant us success, for God gets all the glory. And oh, what wonders has God often done by bruised reeds! Yea, it is the bruised reed that is oftenest the instrument in His hand for working His mighty signs and wonders. What consolation is this! Suffering is stripped of half its bitterness if it thus brings with it a double portion of the Spirit, and fits for double usefulness on earth.

9. *We have the Holy Spirit as our Comforter.* He is mighty to comfort as well as to sanctify. His name is 'the Comforter'. His office is to console. And in the discharge of this office, He puts forth His power, not only *mediately* and indirectly through the Word, but *immediately* and directly upon the soul, sustaining and strengthening it when fainting and troubled. It is consolation unspeakable to know that there is a hand, a divine and omnipotent hand, laid upon our wounded spirit, not only upholding it, but

drying up, as it were, the very springs of grief within. In the day of oppressive sorrow, when bowed down to the dust, what is it that we feel so much our need of as a hand that can come into close and direct contact with our souls to lift them up and strengthen them? For it is here that human consolation fails. Friends can say much to soothe us, but they cannot lay their finger upon the hidden seat of sorrow. They can put their arm around the fainting body, but not around the fainting spirit. To that they have only distant and indirect access. But here the heavenly aid comes in. The Spirit throws around us the everlasting arms, and we are invincibly upheld. We cannot sink, for He sustains, He comforts, He cheers. And who knows so well as He how to sustain, and comfort, and cheer?

*10. The time is short.* We have not a pilgrimage like Seth's or Noah's, or even Abraham's to pass through. Ours is but a handbreadth in comparison with theirs. We have not many days to suffer, nor many nights to watch, even though our whole life were filled with weary days and sleepless nights. 'Our light affliction is but for a moment.' And besides the briefness of our earthly span, we know that the coming of the Lord draweth nigh. This is consolation, for it tells not only of the end of our tribulation, but of the beginning of our triumph; nay, and not only of our individual rest from trouble; but of the rest and deliverance of the whole Church together. For then the whole 'body of Christ,' waking or sleeping, shall be glorified with their glorified Lord, and everlasting joy shall be upon their heads. In the day of bereavement, the day of mourning over those who have fallen asleep in Jesus, this consolation is especially precious. Them that sleep in Jesus will God bring with Him. And if the Lord be near, the time of reunion may not be far off. They that lie down at evening have a whole night's slumber before them; but they who lie down toward morning have, it may be, but an hour or less till the dawn awakes them. So with the dead in Christ in these last days. They will not have long to sleep, for it is now the fourth watch of the night, and the day-star is preparing to arise. What consolation! How it soothes the pain of parting! How it cheers the wounded spirit! 'Awake, and sing, ye that dwell in dust,' is now our watchword every day. We take our stand upon our watchtower, and look out amidst the darkness of night for the first streaks of morn. We lay our ear to the ground and listen that, amid all the discord of earth, the uproar of war, the tumults of the nations, we may catch the first sound of our Lord's chariot wheels – those chariot wheels that are to sweep in vengeance over the field of Armageddon, crushing the confederate nations leagued against the Lord and His Anointed, and also to bring to the bosom of the long betrothed

Bride, the Husband of her youth, the desire of her soul, for whom, amid tears and loneliness, she has waited for many a generation, many a century, in vain.

*11. All is love.* Affliction is the expression of paternal love. It is from the deepest recess of the fountain of love that sorrow flows down to us. And love cannot wrong us. It blesses, but cannot curse. Its utterances and actions are all of peace and gladness. It wants a larger vessel into which to empty itself, and a deeper channel through which to flow. That is all. It seeks to make us more susceptible of kindness, and then to pour that kindness in. Yes, love is the true, the one origin of the sharpest stroke that ever fell upon a bleeding heart. The truth is, there is no other way of accounting for affliction but this. Anger will not account for it, forgetfulness will not account for it, chance will not account for it. No. It is simply impossible to trace it to any cause but love. Admit this as its spring, and all is harmonious, comely, perfect. Deny it, and all is confusion, cruelty, and darkness. Chastising love is the faithfullest, purest, truest, tenderest, deepest of all. Let this be our consolation.

Beloved, 'it is well.' It is *good* to be afflicted. Our days of suffering here we call days of darkness; hereafter they will seem our brightest and fairest. In eternity we shall praise Jehovah most of all for our sorrows and tears. So blessed shall they then seem to us that we shall wonder how we could ever weep and sigh. We shall then know how utterly unworthy we were of all this grace. We did not deserve anything, but least of all to be afflicted. Our joys were all of *grace* – pure grace – much more our sorrows. It is out of the 'exceeding riches of the grace of God' that trial comes.

## 15

# THE ETERNAL RESULTS

'If we suffer we shall also reign with him.' Of this we are assured. Oneness in suffering here is the pledge of oneness in glory hereafter. The two things are inseparable. His shame is ours on earth; His glory shall be ours in Heaven. Therefore, let us 'rejoice, inasmuch as ye are partakers of Christ's sufferings; that, when his glory shall be revealed, ye may be glad also with exceeding joy' (1 Pet. 4:13).

Truly the sufferings of this present life are not worthy to be compared with the glory which shall be revealed in us. The incorruptible crown is so surpassingly bright, and the 'inheritance of the saints in light' so excellent that we may well be ashamed even to speak of present sorrow. How will the eternal light absorb the darkness here! How will the blessedness of the kingdom swallow up our earthly calamities and complaints! One hour of eternity, one moment with the Lord will make us utterly forget a lifetime of desolations. But more than this. Our troubles now do but enhance the coming joy. Our affliction is not only 'light,' not only 'but for a moment,' but it worketh for us a far more exceeding and eternal weight of glory. Our sorrows here are but adding to the weight of our eternal crown. In what way they do so we are not told. It is sufficient that we know upon God's authority that such is really the case. Need we then grudge or rebel against that which is preparing for us such glad and sure results?

As to the nature of the recompense, God has revealed much to us, at least insofar as human language and earthly figures can set it forth. In the epistles to the seven churches of Asia we have the fullest opening of this manifold reward. For 'him that overcometh,' there is an abundant 'weight of glory' provided. To each of the seven conquerors there is a separate reward, and taking them all together, what a fullness of infinite blessing is comprised in this sevenfold recompense! To one conqueror there is promised the 'tree of life'. To another, the 'crown of life' and deliverance from the second death. To another, 'the hidden manna,' the 'white stone,' and in it the new, the unknown name. To another, the honour of being made a pillar in the temple of God, and of having written on him the name of God and the name of his city – God's own new name. To another, a seat upon the throne of Christ, joint dominion with Him in His kingdom, joint heirship with Him in His inheritance, for 'he that overcometh shall inherit all things'.

True, this recompense is only 'to him that

overcometh'. It is a lifetime battle – a wrestling not only with flesh and blood, but with principalities and powers, with the rulers of the darkness of this world, with spiritual wickedness in high places. But then, however desperate the warfare, it is not forever. Nay, it is brief, very brief. Its end is near, very near. And with the end comes triumph, and honour, and songs of victory. Then, too, there follows peace, and the return of the war-worn soldier to his quiet dwelling.

Now the soft peace-march beats,
home, brothers, home.

This is the joy of the saint. He has fought a good fight, he has finished the course, he has kept the faith. Henceforth there is laid up for him the crown of righteousness. His battle is over, and then for him there are rest and home. Home! Yes, home. And what a home for us to return to and abide in forever! A home prepared before the foundation of the world, a home in the many mansions, a home in the innermost circle of creation, nearest the throne and heart of God, a home whose peace shall never be broken by the sound of war or tempest, whose brightness shall never be overcast by the remotest shadow of a cloud. How solacing to the weary spirit to think of a resting-place so near, and that resting-place our Father's house where we shall hunger no more, neither thirst any more, where the sun shall not light on us, nor any heat, where the Lamb that is in the midst of the throne shall feed us and lead us to living fountains of waters, and God shall wipe away all tears from our eyes.

The time is at hand. The Church's conflicts are almost over. Its struggles and sorrows are nearly done. A few more years, and we shall either be laid quietly to rest, or caught up into the clouds to meet our coming Lord. A few more broken bonds, and then we shall be knit together in eternal brotherhood with all the scattered members of the family. A few more suns shall rise and set, and then shall ascend in its strength the one unsetting sun. A few more days shall dawn and darken, and then shall shine forth the one unending day. A few more clouds shall gather over us, and then the firmament shall be cleared forever. A few more sabbaths shall come around, filling the sum of our privileges and completing our allotment of time, and then the everlasting sabbath shall begin. But a few brief years, and we shall 'enter in through the gates into the city,' sitting down beneath the shadow of the tree of life, feeding upon the hidden manna, and drinking of the pure river clear as crystal, which proceedeth out of the throne of God and of the Lamb. But a few years and we shall see His face, and His name shall be upon our foreheads.

These are some of the eternal results, results which are mightily heightened and enhanced by our tribulations here. For affliction not only profits us much just now, but it will serve us much in eternity. Then we shall discover how much we owe to it. All that it is doing for us, we know not now, but we shall know hereafter. It is preparing for us 'more abundant entrance,' a weightier crown, a whiter robe, a sweeter rest, a home made doubly precious by a long exile and many sufferings here below.

Of these results we have only the foretaste now. The full brightness is in reserve, and we know that all that is possible or conceivable of what is good and fair and blessed shall one day be real and visible. Out of all evil there comes the good; out of sin comes holiness; out of darkness, light; out of death, life eternal; out of weakness, strength; out of the fading, the blooming; out of a quenched planet, a sun for the universe; out of rottenness and ruin, comeliness and majesty; out of the curse, the blessing; and *Resurrection* shall prove the wondrous truth that it is the grave – the place of bones and dust – that is the womb of the incorruptible, the immortal, the glorious, the undefiled.

Our present portion, however, is but the earnest, not the inheritance. *That* is reserved for the appearing of the Lord. Here we see but through a glass darkly. It doth not yet appear what we shall be. We are but as wayfaring men, wandering in the lonely night, who see dimly upon the distant mountain peak the reflection of a sun that never rises here, but which shall never set in the 'new heavens' hereafter.

And this is enough. It comforts and cheers us on our dark and rugged way. It would not be enough hereafter, but it is enough just now. The wilderness will do for us till we cross into Canaan. The tent will do till the 'city of habitation' comes. The joy of believing is enough till we enter on the joy of seeing. We are content with the 'mountain of myrrh, and the hill of frankincense,' until 'the day break and the shadows flee away'.

Horatius Bonar (1808-1889) was a minister of the Free Church of Scotland. Today he is best known for his hymns (of which he wrote over 600), but during his lifetime he was also a popular writer. In addition to *Night of Weeping*, Christian Focus publishes Bonar's *Follow The Lamb*, a book suitable for new Christians.